COVENANT

COVENANT
Steven L. McKenzie

INCARNATION
Jon L. Berquist

SABBATH AND JUBILEE
Richard H. Lowery

COVENANT

STEVEN L. McKENZIE

Chalice Press.

St. Louis, Missouri

2000

Cover and interior design: Elizabeth Wright
Art direction: Elizabeth Wright

This book is printed on acid-free, recycled paper.

Visit Chalice Press on the World Wide Web at
www.chalicepress.com

10 9 8 7 6 5 4 3 2 1   00 01 02 03

Library of Congress Cataloging–in–Publication Data

McKenzie, Steven L., 1953–
    Covenant / by Steven L. McKenzie.
        p.   cm. — (Understanding biblical themes)
    Includes bibliographical references and idex.
    ISBN 0-8272-3872-4
    1. Covenants—Biblical teaching.   I. Title.   II. Series.
BS680.C67 M36   2000
231.7'6 — dc21   00-009777
                                                          CIP

Printed in the United States of America

CONTENTS

ABBREVIATIONS

AASF   Annales Academiæ Scientarum Fennicæ

AB   The Anchor Bible

ABD   *The Anchor Bible Dictionary*

ABRL   The Anchor Bible Reference Library

AnBib   Analecta Biblica

ANTC   Abingdon New Testament Commentaries

BA   *The Biblical Archaeologist*

BAR   *Biblical Archaeology Review*

BASOR   *Bulletin of the American Society of Oriental Research*

BibOr   Biblica et Orientalia

BZAW   Beihefte zur *Zeitschrift für die alttestamentliche Wissenschaft*

ConBOT   Coniectanea Biblica, Old Testament

HSM   Harvard Semitic Monographs

HTR   *Harvard Theological Review*

ICC   The International Critical Commentary

Interp *Interpretation*

JAOS	*Journal of the American Oriental Society*
JBL	*Journal of Biblical Literature*
JSNTSup	*Journal for the Study of the New Testament,* Supplement Series
JSOT	*Journal for the Study of the Old Testament*
JSOTSup	*Journal for the Study of the Old Testament,* Supplement Series
NCB	New Century Bible
NTG	New Testament Guides
OBO	Orbis biblicus et orientalis
OBT	Overtures to Biblical Theology
OCB	*Oxford Companion to the Bible*
OTG	Old Testament Guides
OTL	The Old Testament Library
RQ	*Restoration Quarterly*
SBT	Studies in Biblical Theology
TDNT	*Theological Dictionary of the New Testament*
TDOT	*Theological Dictionary of the Old Testament*
TLOT	*Theological Lexicon of the Old Testament*
VT	*Vetus Testamentum*

WBC   Word Biblical Commentary

WMANT Wissenschaftliche Monographien zum Alten und Neuen
          Testament

ZAW   *Zeitschrift für die alttestamentliche Wissenschaft*

INTRODUCTION

The word *covenant* was something of a comfort to me when I bought my first house. Among all the lines of legalese printed on a stack of official documents was a word I finally understood. It occurred repeatedly in several different usages. On the deed of trust from the mortgage company the borrower (me) *covenanted* to being "lawfully seized" of the "estate" I was buying. There was a section of "uniform covenants" that both borrower and lender "covenanted" and agreed to follow. The entire document, in fact, was a "covenant and agreement." The comfort afforded by the word disappeared, however, when I realized that my covenant in the matter was a promise and commitment to pay a large sum of money every month for most of the rest of my life.

These different usages of "covenant" fit the dictionary definition of the word, which is worth quoting in full:

> 1. an agreement, usually formal, between two or more persons to do or not do something specified. 2. *Law.* an incidental clause in such an agreement. 3. *Eccles.* a solemn agreement between the members of a church to act together in harmony with the precepts of the gospel. 4. (*cap.*) *Hist.* a. See **National Covenant.** b. **Solemn League and Covenant.**

1

5. *Bible.* **a.** the conditional promises made to man by God, as revealed in Scripture. **b.** the agreement between God and the ancient Israelites, in which God promised to protect them if they kept His law and were faithful to Him. **6.** *Law.* **a.** a formal agreement of legal validity, esp. one under seal. **b.** an early English form of action in suits involving sealed contracts. **7.** See **Covenant of the League of Nations.** —v.i. **8.** to enter into a covenant. —v.t. **9.** to agree to by covenant; pledge. **10.** to stipulate. [ME < OF, n. use of prp. of *convenir* < L *convenire* to come together, agree] —**Syn. 1.** treaty, pact, convention.[1]

My deed of trust was a formal agreement of legal validity as described in definitions 1 and 6a. It contained various incidental clauses also called covenants, as per definition 2. By signing the deed I was covenanting, entering into an agreement with the mortgage company—definition 8. Specifically, I was stipulating (definition 10) that I was residing on the property and was pledging (definition 9) to repay the loan for the purchase amount. The deed was a mutual agreement or pact—one might even say a contract.

Aside from its use in legal documents, *covenant* today is basically a religious term. I understood what the word meant on my deed, not because of any legal experience, but because of my familiarity with it in the Bible and in religious training. *Covenant* is not commonly used in daily speech; most people prefer a word like *agreement* instead. In the dictionary the meanings of *covenant* in the Bible and in an ecclesiastical (church) setting are prominent. The dictionary also tells something else very important about the word covenant. It explains the word as deriving originally from Latin. But the Bible is written in other languages—primarily Hebrew and Greek, with some Aramaic. The Latin and English words are translations. They come from a different culture and way of thinking than those that produced the Bible, so that something is always "lost in translation." In order to understand what the Bible means by *covenant* we cannot rely solely on translation but must explore the senses of the Hebrew and Greek words as well as the historical, social, and literary contexts in which they occur.

There are two main words—one Hebrew and one Greek—translated "covenant" in the Bible. The Hebrew word, *bʰrît* (ברית),

---

[1] *Webster's Encyclopedic Unabridged Dictionary* (New York: Random House, 1989).

will be familiar to many readers already, though they may not recognize its meaning. It is found in the name of the philanthropic organization of Jewish men, B'nai B'rith, which would most naturally be translated "sons of the covenant." It is also the term used in modern Judaism (pronounced *bris*) for the circumcision of male babies on their eighth day in accordance with God's *covenant* with Abraham in Genesis 17. The etymology of the word is uncertain, but this has little bearing on its usage and meaning in the Bible.[2]

The Greek word used in the New Testament for covenant is really a translation of *b'rît*. The word is *diathēkē* (διαθηκη), which actually means "last will" or "testament." When the Hebrew Bible was translated into Greek in the work known as the Septuagint (abbreviated LXX), *diathēkē* was the word used to render *b'rît*, "covenant." The writers of the New Testament inherited the word and also used *diathēkē* when they spoke of covenant. It is from this set of circumstances that the Old and New Testaments received their names.

Defining "covenant" in the Bible, especially *b'rît*, is not as easy as it might seem. Broadly, the word refers to an arrangement of some kind between two or more parties. But the exact nature of the arrangement is not always clear. The dictionary definitions of the term in the Bible refer to God's promises but imply that there is an obligation of obedience or faithfulness upon which the promises are conditioned. So to what extent is "covenant" in the Bible promissory, and to what extent does it represent an obligation? Are both parties obligated or just one? Is the biblical covenant imposed by one party on another, or are its terms negotiated and arrived at by mutual consent and agreement? Is a covenant in the Bible always between two parties, or can it involve more than two? These are the kinds of questions that we shall try to address in this book.

---

[2]Five suggestions for the etymology of *b'rît* have been offered: (1) < *brh* I, "to eat," reflecting the practice of a meal as part of a covenant-making ceremony; (2) < *brh* II, "to see," with the derived meanings "to choose, decide" for the verb and hence "decision, decree, obligation" for the noun; (3) < *birît*, a preposition meaning "between" found in Akkadian (Babylonian) but not in Hebrew; (4) < *birtu*, an Akkadian word for "clasp, fetter" and hence for "bond"; (5) < *br*, a root meaning "set apart," so that a covenant is a specially designated or set-apart favor or benefit. For further discussion see James Barr, "Some Semantic Notes on Covenant," in Herbert Donner, Robert Hanhart, and Rudolf Smend, eds., *Beiträge zur alttestamentlichen Theologie: Festschrift für Walther Zimmerli zum 70. Geburtstag* (Göttingen: Vandenhoeck & Ruprecht, 1977), 23–38; Ernest W. Nicholson, *God and His People: Covenant and Theology in the Old Testament* (Oxford: Clarendon Press, 1986), 94–103; and Moshe Weinfeld, "ברית berîth," *TDOT*, 2:253–55.

An Overview of Covenants in the Bible

The Bible describes many distinct covenants between different parties. An overview of these will be useful as a foundation for further study. A leading lexicon of ancient Hebrew divides the occurrences of *bᵉrît* into two categories—those to which God is a party and those involving only humans.[3] For the sake of convenience I shall follow this same division.

Covenants between God and Humans

Some interpreters have perceived Adam and Eve as living under a covenant in Genesis 2—3. However, the first occurrence of the word *bᵉrît* in the Bible is in the Noah story, where God "establishes" a covenant first with Noah (Gen. 6:18) and then with all the survivors of the flood, animals as well as humans (Gen. 9:9–10). Next, God made (literally "cut"—we will discuss this expression later) a covenant with Abraham and his descendants ("seed," Gen. 15:18; 17:7). This covenant was the foundation for God's further relationship with Israel. It was passed on to Isaac and Jacob, and it served as God's motivation for rescuing the Hebrews from Egyptian bondage. "God heard their groaning, and God remembered his covenant with Abraham, with Isaac, and with Jacob" (Exod. 2:24; cf. 6:4–5). It also provided the motive for Yahweh not to allow Israel to be completely destroyed when they sinned (2 Kgs. 13:23), but to restore them to their land once they repented (Lev. 26:40–45).

By far the most prominent covenant in the Hebrew Bible is the one mediated by Moses between God and Israel. This is the one considered *the* Old Testament covenant. Some passages, such as Leviticus 26:42–45, mentioned earlier, see this as a continuation of the covenant with the patriarchs. This covenant takes place in stages. Exodus 24:3–8 recounts a covenant-making ceremony in which the people agree to keep the stipulations of the "book of the covenant" that Moses has read to them (24:7). Moses then goes up to Mount Sinai to receive the two tablets of stone upon which God has written his commands. These are later called the "tablets of the covenant" (31:18; 32:15), although the word *covenant* here is not *bᵉrît* but another word

---

[3]Francis Brown, S. R. Driver, and Charles A. Briggs, *A Hebrew and English Lexicon of the Old Testament* (Oxford: Clarendon Press, 1974), 136–37.

usually translated "testimony." When Moses comes down from the mountain and sees the golden calf constructed by the people in his absence, he throws the tablets down and breaks them (32:1–19). At a second stage, therefore, Moses cuts two more tablets of stone (34:1) upon which God writes the "words of the covenant [*bᵉrît*]"—here identified as the Ten Commandments—that he has made with Israel (34:27–28). The third stage of this covenant takes place in the book of Deuteronomy, which is set on the plains of Moab just east of the Jordan River, as the people prepare to enter the land of Canaan. Here Moses reviews the law (*Deuteronomy* is Greek for "second law") and, according to Deuteronomy 29:1 (Heb. 28:69), makes a covenant between Yahweh and Israel "besides the covenant he made ['cut'] with them at Horeb" (Deuteronomy's name for Sinai). Joshua's mediation of a covenant between God and Israel (Josh. 24:25) might be considered a further extension or renewal of the Mosaic covenant, or at least of the commitment to worship Yahweh exclusively.

Other specialized covenants between God and individual members of the exodus generation include the "covenant of salt" with Aaron and his descendants as Yahweh's priests (Num. 18:19) and the "covenant of peace" and of "perpetual priesthood" with Aaron's grandson, Phinehas, and his descendants because of his zealous deed on Yahweh's behalf (Num. 25:12–13).

The next covenant between God and humans in the Bible is the one with David. Second Samuel 7 (1 Chr. 17), which recounts God's promise to David of an eternal (or enduring) dynasty, does not use the word *bᵉrît*. But other texts, especially in Psalms, refer to this episode as a *bᵉrît* (2 Sam. 23:5; Jer. 33:21; Pss. 89:3, 19–37, 39 [Heb. 89:4, 20–38, 40]; 132:11). The Davidic covenant looms large in the Bible's history of the monarchy as an explanation for the endurance of the nation of Judah, which was David's home tribe. But its language of an "eternal covenant" also raises questions about what is meant by "forever." Other kings of Judah also have covenants with Yahweh, though not of the same nature as David's. The boy king Joash is made party by his guardian to a covenant between God, the people, and himself (2 Kgs. 11:17; 2 Chr. 23:3). In Chronicles' version of Hezekiah's reign, the king expresses his intention to make a covenant with God in an address to the priests and Levites (2 Chr. 29:10). Then King Josiah and all the people make a covenant "before

Yahweh" in 2 Kings 23:1–3. Although Yahweh is not named here as a party to the covenant, the event is occasioned by the finding of the "book of the covenant" and is therefore a renewal of the Mosaic covenant between God and Israel. The covenant effected by Ezra between the returned exiles and "our God" (Ezra 10:3) is very similar to those made by kings, though it takes place after the end of the monarchy. This covenant also may be thought of as a renewal of the Mosaic one, since the people agree to put away their foreign wives and children in accordance with (their interpretation of) Mosaic legislation.

In addition to these historical narratives, the prophetic books contain a series of references to covenants. Whether Hosea refers to an existing covenant between God and Israel is disputed. The covenants in Hosea 6:7 and especially 8:1 could be the Mosaic covenant or covenants between people or nations. The (chronologically) later prophets, Jeremiah (11:1–10; 14:21; 22:9; 31:32) and Ezekiel (16:8, 59–61), do mention Yahweh's covenant with Israel, and in Jeremiah 11:1–10 this is clearly the Mosaic covenant with the exodus generation. More common in the prophets is the reference to God's establishment of a covenant with Israel in the future. Several passages envision such a covenant and describe not so much how the covenant will be different, but how the attitude of the people will change (Isa. 55:3; 59:21; Jer. 31:31, 33; 32:40; 50:5; Ezek. 16:60, 62; 20:37; 34:25; 37:26; Hos. 2:18 [Heb. 2:20]). Only Jeremiah 31 refers to this as a "new" covenant, but all these texts agree in describing this covenant as enduring "forever."

In the New Testament, Jesus is seen as establishing a new covenant through his blood, as he mentions in the institution of the eucharist at the Last Supper (Matt. 26:28; Mark 14:24; Luke 22:20; 1 Cor. 11:25). The image of ratifying a covenant through blood in these passages and elsewhere in the New Testament (Heb. 10:29; 12:24; 13:20) is borrowed from the covenant-making ceremony in the Hebrew Bible (Exod. 24:8). The New Testament writers recognize the plurality of covenants in the Hebrew Bible (Rom. 9:4; Eph. 2:12). They trace God's covenant with Israel back to Abraham and seem to see the Sinai covenant as continuous with, or subsumed under, the Abrahamic one (Acts 3:25; 7:8; Gal. 3:15 [where there is an intriguing play on the sense of *diathēkē* as testament], 17; 4:24 [where Hagar is interpreted as an allegory for Mount Sinai!]). In addition to Galatians

4:24, other texts also seem to identify the covenant in the Hebrew Bible as the law (2 Cor. 3:6, 14). Second Corinthians 3 contrasts the covenants in the Hebrew Bible and New Testament as old and new, letter and spirit, and even death and life. The book of Hebrews draws this contrast at length and is particularly concerned with trying to demonstrate the superority of the "new" covenant in Christ over the "old" covenant under the law of the Hebrew Bible. However, in Romans 9 Paul seems to argue that the covenant with Israel was never abrogated, but is still in effect. This relationship between the covenant(s) in the Hebrew Bible and the New Testament is one that we will consider in detail in later chapters.

Covenants between Human Beings

In this book we are primarily interested in the covenants between God and humans. However, covenants between people are important for the light they shed on the nature and variety of covenants in general. The patriarchs made covenants with other people: Abraham with his Amorite "allies" in Genesis 14:13 (NRSV, literally "owners of the covenant with Abraham") and with Abimelech (Gen. 21:27), Isaac also with Abimelech (Gen. 26:26–31), and Jacob with Laban (Gen. 31:44–50). The Israelites under Joshua make an ill-advised covenant (NRSV, "treaty") with the Gibeonites (Josh. 9:3–21) in violation of the prohibition against covenant making with the indigenous population of Canaan (Exod. 23:32; 34:12, 15; Deut. 7:2). Amos' reference to a "covenant of brothers" between Tyre and Edom (1:9) illustrates the use of kinship language for covenant or treaty partners that was typical in the ancient Near East.

The account of the monarchy contains references to a number of covenants, most of which are between political entities. When threatened by the Ammonite king Nahash, the people of Jabesh-gilead tried to negotiate a covenant (1 Sam. 11:1). David and Jonathan made a covenant (1 Sam. 18:3); like most treaties and covenants between people, it is sworn before the deity (23:18) and is therefore called a "covenant of Yahweh" (20:8). David also made covenants with Abner (2 Sam. 3:12–13) and with the elders of Israel (2 Sam. 3:21; 5:3), the latter also "before Yahweh." Solomon had a covenant with Hiram (1 Kings 5:13 [Heb. 5:26]); Baasha of Israel and Asa of Judah both had covenants with Ben-Hadad I of Damascus (1 Kgs. 15:21, "alliance"); and a later king of Israel (Ahab) had a covenant with a later

Ben-Hadad (II) (1 Kgs. 20:34). The Assyrians probably had a covenant affirming Israel's vassalhood, against which they rebelled. While 2 Kings 17:3–4 does not used the word "covenant," Hosea 12:1 [Heb. 12:2] mentions a covenant with Assyria, and Hosea condemns the Israelites for breaking this, and perhaps other, covenants with people (Hos. 10:4; cf. 6:7). The Babylonians had such a covenant with Judah—sworn "before Yahweh" and therefore considered "my covenant" by Yahweh, who promised to punish Judah for breaking it (Ezek. 17:11–21). Similarly, King Zedekiah's covenant with the people of Jerusalem to release their Hebrew slaves was also Yahweh's covenant, because it had been sworn before him so that he would punish those who broke it for profaning his name (Jer. 34:8–20).

In addition to these covenants between political entities, the Bible also refers in a few passages to marriage as a covenant. Again, this covenant is sworn "before Yahweh" so that he is a witness to it (Mal. 2:14), and that makes marriage a sacred covenant (Prov. 2:17). In Hosea 1—3 Hosea's own marriage is used as a metaphor for God's relationship with Israel, although neither the marriage nor the relationship is explicitly called a "covenant" (but 2:18 does refer to a new covenant that Yahweh will make between Israel and "nature" in the context of the remarriage of God and Israel).

Finally, there are a couple of covenants mentioned in the Bible in which one of the parties is neither Yahweh nor a human. In asserting his innocence in the face of his suffering, Job (31:1) states that he has made a covenant with his eyes not even to look at a virgin so as not to be tempted to sexual sin. Also, Isaiah 28:15 quotes the leaders of Jerusalem as claiming that they have a "covenant with death" that will allow them to escape annihilation when it comes upon the city; in verse 18 Yahweh declares that this covenant with death will be voided.

The Importance of Covenant in the Bible

It is clear from the preceding survey that covenant is the principal image used in the Bible to express the relationship between God and humans. This applies to more than just the Israelites. Whether the Bible describes a covenant between God and Adam and Eve is something we shall have to investigate. However, there is definitely a covenant between God and Noah in the Bible that applies to all people and serves as the foundation for future relationships. In addition to the main covenant in the Hebrew Bible, the one with Israel at Sinai, the image of covenant is used for other (promissory) arrangements that God makes with individuals—such as the covenants with Aaron, Phinehas, and David. In the New Testament the image of covenant continues to be used for the relationship mediated by Christ and available to persons of all ethnic origins and national backgrounds.

More to the point, covenant is the main biblical image for the distinctive relationship of the people of Israel with God. The theological significance of covenant in the Hebrew Bible has long been recognized: "'Covenant' is the central expression of the distinctive faith of Israel as 'the people of Yahweh,' children of God by adoption and free decision rather than by nature or necessity."[4] "Covenant is the concept in which Israelite thought gave definitive expression to the binding of the people to God and by means of which they established firmly from the start the particularity of their knowledge of him was the covenant."[5]

The second quotation is from a two-volume work on the theology of the Old Testament that treats covenant as the central concept around which its entire theological message is constructed. It is evident from just these two quotations that election, faith(fulness), obedience, and the law are some of the important theological concepts in the constellation that orbits around covenant. We shall investigate some of these concepts in relationship to covenant later in this book.

The preservation of the Hebrew word for covenant in present-day institutions such as the B'nai B'rith and the *bris,* as we noted above, suggests the extent to which covenant continues to form a part of Jewish self-identity. The fact that Christians see themselves as people of the New "Testament" indicates that covenant forms an important part of their self-identity as well. An understanding of covenant, therefore, is crucial for any discussion of the relationship of Judaism and Christianity to each other; their relationship is based on that of the respective covenants of the Hebrew Bible and New Testament. This relationship is difficult to characterize, but its importance will demand our full attention later in this book. The importance of covenant for Judaism and Christianity as suggested by these features is the motivation for our detailed study of covenant in the Bible, to which we now turn.

---

[4]Nicholson, *God and His People,* viii.
[5]Walther Eichrodt, *Theology of the Old Testament,* vol. I, OTL, trans. J. A. Baker (Philadelphia: Westminster Press, 1961), 36.

1

FAMILY TIES
The Origins of Covenant in Israel

We do not know exactly when and where the idea of covenant arose in Israel. The best possibility is that it developed as an extension of family relationships even before there was an Israel.[1] In the world of ancient Israel, society was organized along kinship lines.[2] The basic unit was the extended family, called "the house of the father" (Hebrew *bêt 'āv*), followed by the clan (*mishpāḥāh*), and then the tribe (*shevet* or *maṭṭeh*). Clans and especially tribes established alliances with other such units through covenants or treaties in which they took oaths before their gods to follow certain guidelines or accept certain responsibilities relating to each other. The covenant was, therefore, a cultural, legal, and religious

---

[1]For much of this subsection I am indebted to Frank Moore Cross, "Kinship and Covenant in Ancient Israel," in *From Epic to Canon: History and Literature in Ancient Israel* (Baltimore/London: Johns Hopkins University Press, 1998), 3–21.

[2]On the social organization of early Israel see Lawrence E. Stager, "The Archaeology of the Family in Ancient Israel," *BASOR* 260 (1985): 1–29.

11

device for uniting distinct kinship groups. Such covenants were often recorded in writing for future reference.

The alliance as represented by a covenant was a way of incorporating outsiders into a kinship group. Thus, the language and imagery of family relations were carried over into covenants and treaties. They were often sealed by marriages. In the Bible (1 Kgs. 11:1–3) Solomon is said to have had seven hundred wives who were foreign princesses, a statement that indicates the extent of his international treaties. The term "marriage alliance" in 1 Kings 3:1 (NRSV), used of Solomon's marriage to Pharaoh's daughter, literally means "to become son-in-law." The treaty partners referred to each other as "brothers" or, in the case of an overlord and vassal, "father" and "son," respectively. Thus, in 1 Kings 20:32–34 the king of Israel calls the king of Aram (Syria), whom he has just defeated in battle, his "brother" as a conciliatory gesture meant to emphasize their equality. The Syrian king immediately offers a set of concessions, and the two kings make a treaty (v. 34).

The Bible describes the relationships among the tribes of Israel in terms of kinship, not of covenants. That is, it describes the nation of Israel as made up of twelve tribes, which are descended from twelve brothers, who were all sons of one father named Jacob or Israel. But the kinship language may actually reflect covenantal ties between the tribes rather than ties of blood. This would mean that ancient Israel was a confederation of independent tribes bound together by a covenant sworn before Yahweh. It was this covenant that united them as "brothers" within a single family—the people of Yahweh. There are certain biblical texts that suggest an understanding of Israel along these lines. We will examine two of these.

The "Song of Deborah"

The "Song of Deborah" in Judges 5 is one of the oldest, if not *the* oldest, single passage in the Hebrew Bible. It is poetry and is set in Deborah's mouth in celebration of Israel's victory over their Canaanite foe, King Jabin, and his general, Sisera, which is recounted in the preceeding chapter. In actuality, the old poem in chapter 5 has been interpreted and elaborated by the prose story in chapter 4.[3] This is

---

[3]On the direction of borrowing see Baruch Halpern, "Sisera and Old Lace: The Case of Deborah and Yael," in *The First Historians: The Hebrew Bible and History* (San Francisco: Harper & Row, 1988), esp. 76–82.

evident from a comparison of the two versions of Sisera's death. In 5:26 ("She put her hand to the tent peg and her right hand to the workmen's mallet," NRSV), "tent peg" and "workmen's mallet" are poetic variants, as are "hand" and "right hand." This kind of "parallelism"—saying the same thing or similar things in two different lines—is the hallmark of Hebrew poetry. The point is that Jael used an everyday tool to strike Sisera on the head *as he stood* so that he fell dead at her feet (5:27). The author of the prose has interpreted this literally so that Jael uses *both* the tent peg and the mallet to kill Sisera, nailing his head to the ground as he sleeps (4:21).

The poem begins with a description of Yahweh marching forth as the divine warrior, apparently to do battle on behalf of his people (5:4–5). The part that is of most interest to us at present is the list of tribes that were summoned to go to war under the leadership of Deborah and Barak (vv. 12–18). They fall into two categories: the six tribes that responded to the summons and joined Deborah and Barak (Ephraim, Benjamin, Machir, Zebulun, Issachar, and Naphtali, vv. 14–15a, 18) and the four that stayed behind (Reuben, Gilead, Dan, Asher, vv. 15b–17).[4] The list differs markedly from the usual list of the tribes or sons of Israel in the Bible:

Standard list	Judges 5
Reuben	Reuben (v. 15b–16)
Simeon	
Levi	
Judah	
Dan	Dan (v. 17aβ)
Naphtali	Naphtali (v. 18b)
Gad	
Asher	Asher (v. 17b)
Issachar	Issachar (v. 15a)
Zebulun	Zebulun (v. 14bβ, 18a)
Ephraim	Ephraim (v. 14aα)
Manasseh	
Benjamin	Benjamin (v. 14aβ)
	Machir (v. 14bα)
	Gilead (v. 17aα)

---

[4]In addition to the article by Stager cited above, see his "The Song of Deborah: Why Some Tribes Answered the Call and Others Did Not," *BAR* 15, no. 1 (Jan./Feb. 1989): 51–64.

The "standard list" is based on four passages: Genesis 29:31—30:24; Genesis 49; Numbers 1—2; and Joshua 13—22. The order of the tribes in these lists varies for reasons that lie outside our present concerns. The order followed here is that of Genesis 29:31—30:24, which we shall discuss momentarily. The essential content of the lists is identical.[5] This makes the list in Judges 5 all the more remarkable for its differences. In the first place, Judges 5 lists only ten tribes, not twelve (or thirteen with Levi). Missing are Simeon, Levi, Judah, Gad, and Manasseh. The absence of Levi might be explained because it is the priestly tribe and owns no land; but the others should be included within a full list of the tribes of Israel. Moreover, there are tribes listed in Judges 5 that are not included in the standard list elsewhere. Machir and Gilead appear elsewhere as clans within Manasseh (Josh. 17) but not as independent tribes. The list in Judges 5, therefore, suggests that the makeup of Israel changed over time as more clans and tribes were incorporated into the "people of Yahweh," presumably through covenant. The number and identity of the tribes of Israel did not become fixed until some point after the Song of Deborah.

Genesis 29:31—30:24

Careful consideration of the story of the birth of Jacob's sons in Genesis 29:31—30:24 also indicates that the relationship of the Israelite tribes was social, rather than familial. In this story the patriarchs of the twelve tribes are said to have been fathered by Jacob through four women: the sisters Leah and Rachel and their respective handmaidens, Zilpah and Bilhah.

In the story, God sees that Jacob loves Rachel more than Leah and compensates by giving Leah children while Rachel is initially barren. Leah bears Reuben, Simeon, Levi, and Judah. When Rachel realizes that she is barren, she gives her handmaid, Bilhah, to Jacob, and Bilhah bears Dan and Naphtali. Leah, who has ceased to bear, responds by giving her handmaid also, and Zilpah bears Gad and Asher. Leah's childbearing ability is temporarily restored by mandrakes, a plant considered to possess aphrodisiac and fertility properties, so that she bears Issachar and Zebulun. Finally, God remembers Rachel and allows her to conceive and bear Joseph, whose two sons, Ephraim

---

[5]Genesis 29:31—30:24, which recounts the birth of Jacob's sons, does not actually mention Ephraim and Manasseh because they are considered the sons of Joseph and are not yet born. It also does not mention Benjamin, who is also born later and whose mother, Rachel, dies in childbirth (Gen. 35:15–21).

and Manasseh, generate tribes of their own. Later on (Gen. 35:15–21), Rachel dies giving birth to her final son, Benjamin. The ultimate result may be diagrammed as follows:

Leah	*Bilhah*	*Zilpah*	*Rachel*
Reuben	Dan	Gad	Joseph
Simeon	Naphtali	Asher	(Benjamin)
Levi			
Judah			
Issachar			
Zebulun			

The fictional nature of the story is indicated by reflection on the motif of the handmaid. This motif occurs earlier in Genesis (16:1–2) when Sarai insists that Abram take her handmaid, Hagar, in order to produce an heir. Parallels from other ancient Near Eastern texts, especially marriage contracts, show that this was an accepted practice in marriages where a wife failed to produce an heir. But this is clearly not the issue in the story of Jacob's sons, since his first wife, Leah, bears heirs from the beginning. Rather, in that story the motif of the handmaid has been used for a literary purpose, as a creative way of distributing the twelve sons among four mothers. There is, in fact, nothing else in the ancient Near East like the handmaid motif in the Jacob story. The story is not historical and may not have been intended as such. It functions, rather, to explain the social relationship of the tribes of Israel in kinship terms.

We should be clear about how these two texts—the Song of Deborah and the story of the birth of Jacob's sons—relate to the topic of covenant. Both texts indicate that the tribes that constituted Israel were not united by blood but by some social mechanism. There is no explicit mention of covenant as that mechanism, and we have no version of such a federation-forming covenant from the Bible or ancient Israel. The idea, therefore, is speculative. However, the possibility that such a covenant existed remains a good one, particularly considering the common use of kinship language in the ancient Near East to express covenantal relationships. If so, this confederation of tribes as Yahweh's people and under his aegis *may* represent the beginning of covenant in Israel. Still, this kind of covenant is different from the ones presented in the Bible in which God himself is one of the covenantal partners.

Old Covenants with Abraham and on Sinai?

The Bible as it now stands presents covenant as the foundation of Israel's relationship with God from the beginning. Yahweh made a covenant with Abraham and then later with Israel through Moses. But careful readers of the Bible have long recognized that the biblical books are not in chronological order, and the story it presents does not necessarily reflect the actual history of the nation and people of Israel. This is not a criticism of the Bible's message, but simply an observation about its development. Covenant is a good example. The relationship between God and Israel that the covenant represented was an old one, and the covenant was such a fitting image that it seemed perfectly appropriate to use it from the beginning of the story. However, the image of covenant for God's relationship to Israel came to full expression relatively late in Israel's history.

Scholars have long theorized that the first five books of the Bible—Genesis, Exodus, Leviticus, Numbers, and Deuteronomy (also known collectively as the Pentateuch)—are composite. In its classic form, this theory (called the "documentary hypothesis") posits four different authors or written sources behind these books:[6]

> 1. the Yahwist, abbreviated "J" because he[7] used the name Yahweh (German *Jahwe*) for God from the start; dated tenth to ninth century; from Judah

---

[6]For an explanation of this hypothesis and recent criticisms of it see Pauline A. Viviano, "Source Criticism," in Steven L. McKenzie and Stephen R. Haynes, eds., *To Each Its Own Meaning: An Introduction to Biblical Criticisms and Their Application,* rev. ed. (Louisville, Ky.: Westminster John Knox Press, 1999), 35–57; and John Van Seters, "The Pentateuch," in Steven L. McKenzie and M. Patrick Graham, *The Hebrew Bible Today: An Introduction to Critical Issues* (Louisville, Ky.: Westminster John Knox Press, 1998), 3–49. There are a few passages, especially in the Tetrateuch, that mention the covenant and have typically been dated before the eighth century (e.g., Gen. 15:18; Ex. 19:5; 23:32; 24:7–8; 34:10, 27, 28). However, in recent years the early dating of these passages and the sources they represent have consistently come under fire.

[7]All four writers were almost certainly males to judge from the patriarchal content of the Pentateuch as a whole and from what we know of education in the ancient Near East, which was limited for the most part to males (see James L. Crenshaw, *Education in Ancient Israel: Across the Deadening Silence* [ABRL; New York: Doubleday, 1998], esp. 15–18). Richard E. Friedman (*Who Wrote the Bible?* [Englewood Cliffs, N.J.: Prentice-Hall, 1987], 85–86) and Harold Bloom (*The Book of J* [New York: Grove Weidenfeld, 1990]) have recently suggested that J was a woman. Bloom's book reflects a profound ignorance of the biblical world and literature and cannot be taken seriously. Also, Bloom fails to credit Friedman with this idea even though Friedman clearly published it first. Friedman admits that it is unlikely that J was a woman, given educational practices in ancient Israel, but he does not want to exclude the possibility. However, his suggestion is based on the assumption that J was a member of David's court, and this is far from certain.

2. the Elohist, abbreviated "E" because he used the term *'elōhîm* for God; dated ninth to eighth century; from Israel

3. the author of Deuteronomy, abbreviated "D"; dated the late seventh century; work limited to Deuteronomy; incorporated into the "Deuteronomistic History" (Deuteronomy plus Joshua, Judges, 1 and 2 Samuel, 1 and 2 Kings) in the late seventh or early sixth century

4. the priestly writer, abbreviated "P"; dated sixth to fifth century

Most of the references to a covenant between God and Israel in the Pentateuch occur in sections assigned to P or to the Deuteronomistic historian. Both of these writers probably worked in the Babylonian exile (ca. 586–539 B.C.E.), which represented the end of the history of Israel and Judah as nations. Hence, these writings contain elaborations of the covenant idea but not its origin. We will deal with their understanding of covenant in subsequent chapters.

There are only three passages in the Pentateuch that refer to the covenant between God and Israel and that are not in P or the Deuteronomistic History. If these passages are indeed ancient, they would be the oldest mentions of *the* covenant in the Bible. Unfortunately, the dates of all three are disputed, so they require special attention.

Genesis 15

This chapter is crucial for understanding the background to at least one facet of covenant in the Bible. The Hebrew idiom for making a covenant used by many of the biblical writers is literally "to cut a covenant." Genesis 15 illustrates the reason for this idiom. In covenant-making ceremonies, animals were often slaughtered and *cut* to pieces or dismembered as symbols of what would happen to the covenant partner who violated the covenant agreement. As they swore their oaths, the partners would invoke the curses upon themselves by saying something like, "May I, like this animal, be killed if I violate the stipulations of this covenant." That is, in effect, what Yahweh does in this episode. Yahweh is the one making the commitment to Abram, so it is he, represented by the smoking firepot and flaming torch, who passes between the animal pieces. The ritual is very ancient, but it also continued to be practiced over centuries and even millennia. The closest parallels to its description in Genesis 15 are those from later periods. It is only in these later descriptions of the ritual, especially Jeremiah 34:18–19, that the animals are actually cut in half.[8]

In addition to the parallels of dividing the animals in a covenant ritual, there are other features of Genesis 15 that scholars have pointed to recently as indications of its relatively late date.[9] The chapter is dependent on the prophetic literature of the Hebrew Bible in its use of the expression "the word of Yahweh came to" (vv. 1, 4) as well as in its reference to a "vision" (v. 1), which is especially similar to the prophet Ezekiel (sixth century). Abram's name for God, "Yahweh God" (Gen. 15:2, 8), occurs predominately in the prophets (257 of 280 uses in the Hebrew Bible), especially Ezekiel (216 uses). In particular, our chapter is dependent on Jeremiah 34:18–19 in its reference to dividing animals in the covenant ritual[10] and on Isaiah 7:1–17 in its reassurance ("do not fear," v. 1) and its emphasis on faith. Genesis 15 borrows its promises of descendants like the stars and of the dimensions of the promised land from Deuteronomy and the Deuteronomistic History (descendants—Deut. 1:10; 10:22; 28:62; land—Deut. 1:7; 7:1; 9:1; 12:8). Finally, the lateness of the chapter is also indicated by the use of the expression "Ur of the Chaldeans" in 15:7, which presupposes the period when the Chaldeans dominated the Babylonian empire in the second half of the sixth century.[11]

---

[8]See the discussions by John Van Seters, *Abraham in History and Tradition* (New Haven/London: Yale University Press, 1975), 102–3; and John Ha, *Genesis 15: A Theological Compendium of Pentateuchal History* (BZAW 181; Berlin/New York: Walter de Gruyter, 1989), 71–73. The closest parallel to Genesis 15 outside of the Bible is an eighth-century Aramaic inscription from Sefire, which Ha strangely neglects. See Joseph A. Fitzmyer, *The Aramaic Inscriptions of Sefire* (BibOr 19; Rome: Pontifical Biblical Institute, 1967). See also the objections by Richard S. Hess, "The Slaughter of the Animals in Genesis 15," in Richard Hess, Gordon J. Wenham, and P. E. Satterthwaite, eds., *He Swore an Oath: Biblical Themes from Genesis 12—50* (Grand Rapids, Mich.: Baker, 1992), 55–65.

[9]The following points are drawn from the works by Van Seters and Ha cited in the previous note.

[10]The direction of dependence—Genesis 15 dependent on Jeremiah rather than the other way around—is further indicated by the other prophetic language in Genesis 15 and by the fact that Jeremiah refers to the patriarchs only once, in 33:26, which is a very late addition (see chapter 5). Van Seters (*Abraham in History and Tradition*, 264) observes that for Jeremiah (and Ezekiel) the election of Israel took place at the exodus. The transfer of election back to Abraham developed later, in the exile or beyond.

[11]This assumes that Genesis 15 is a unit. While this assumption has been contested, Ha and Van Seters, as well as other recent scholars, have defended it. Ha argues that Genesis 15, especially in vv. 13–16, reflects a knowledge of the Pentateuch as a whole in more or less its finished state and dates the chapter after P at the end of the sixth century or later.

We will say more about the content of the covenant in Genesis 15, especially its promissory nature, in a later chapter. The point for the time being is that despite its placement in the first book of the Bible, this chapter was written at a rather late point in the development of the Hebrew Bible, so that its covenant cannot be seen as the origin of that idea in the Bible or in ancient Israel.

Exodus 19—24

These chapters recount Israel's arrival at Mount Sinai and Moses' reception of the first installments of the law there. The covenant between Yahweh and Israel is referred to three times: 19:5 mentions the rewards accruing to the Israelites if they keep "my covenant"; 24:7–8 forms part of the description of a covenant-making ceremony (vv. 4–8) in which Moses reads the "book of the covenant" (v. 7) and sprinkles the "blood of the covenant" upon the people, either to consecrate them or perhaps, like the dividing of the animals, as a reminder of the consequences of breaking the covenant. Between chapters 19 and 24 are two corpora of laws—the Ten Commandments in 20:1–17 and the "Covenant Code" in 20:22—23:33, so called because of the reference to the book of the covenant in 24:7.

The Ten Commandments may be very old (but see the further discussions in chapters 3 and 9). Scholars have also typically seen the Covenant Code as ancient (though this position, too, has recently been questioned).[12] It is important to recognize, therefore, that neither of these documents identifies itself as a covenant or even mentions a covenant between God and Israel. It is only the story around these documents that refers to them as covenants.

The passages in which the references to covenant occur are dependent on Deuteronomy and the Deuteronomistic History, which dates them no earlier than the end of the seventh century (see chapter 2). As we will see in the next chapter, the "book of the covenant" in 2 Kings 22—23 refers to an early form of the book of Deuteronomy that was the guide for King Josiah's reform. The "book of the covenant" in Exodus 24:7 does not play the same crucial role; the author has borrowed the expression, but not its significance or its content. As for Exodus 19:5, its context (vv. 3–8) is full of Deuteronomic and

---

[12]See John Van Seters, *The Life of Moses: The Yahwist as Historian in Exodus–Numbers* (Louisville: Westminster/John Knox Press, 1994), 247–89.

Deuteronomistic language.[13] For instance, the statement, "You have seen what I did to the Egyptians" (19:4) is similar to exhortations throughout Deuteronomy to remember Yahweh's previous deeds on Israel's behalf (Deut. 4:3, 9; 7:18–19; 10:21–22; 11:7; esp. 29:2 [Heb. 29:1]; Josh. 23:3). The reference to bearing Israel on eagles' wings draws on the image in Deuteronomy 32:11. The term "special property" or "treasured possession" (NRSV) in reference to Israel (v. 5) is especially characteristic of Deuteronomy. It occurs with the word "people" in Deuteronomy 7:6; 14:2; 26:18; and only twice more with this sense (besides Exod. 19:5) in the entire Hebrew Bible (Ps. 135:4; Mal. 3:17). In addition to language, the ideology of these verses fits well with Deuteronomy's message, especially the emphasis on obedience to the covenant and on the election of Israel as Yahweh's people.[14] Finally, the position of Exodus 19:3–8 is odd. The people are commanded to obey the covenant before its stipulations have been given! This is probably because the writer is following the order of Deuteronomy 4—5, where exhortation to obedience also precedes the law code. The difference is that in Deuteronomy this order makes sense because the entire book is cast as a renewal of the covenant given on Sinai (again see chapter 2).[15]

As with Genesis 15, the setting of Exodus 19—24 as a covenant is relatively late and dependent on Deuteronomy and cannot, therefore, be seen as the origin of the idea of the covenant between God and Israel.

Exodus 34

Like Exodus 19—24, chapter 34 contains references to the covenant between God and Israel (vv. 10, 27–28) with legal material in between.[16] But this chapter is not an independent unit. It tells how

---

[13]More details may be found in Lothar Perlitt, *Bundestheologie im Alten Testament* (WMANT 36; Neukirchen: Neukirchener Verlag, 1969), 170–75.

[14]The expressions "priestly kingdom" and "holy nation" in Exodus 19:6 are not common to Deuteronomy or the Deuteronomistic History and suggest that the author of 19:3–8 was not identical to the writer(s) of those works but someone else who drew on them along with other biblical works.

[15]This observation is that of Van Seters, *The Life of Moses*, 272–73.

[16]There are also references in 31:18; 32:15; 34:29 to "the two tablets of the covenant." These expressions use a different word for covenant that is typical of the priestly writer (see chapter 3). This exact expression, "tablets of the covenant," is not found elsewhere in the Hebrew Bible and marks this section off as a unit. Some have seen the legal material in this section as a ritual or cultic version of the Ten Commandments because of the statement in 34:28. But no one has succeeded in dividing it into ten sections, and the meaning of the reference in 34:28 remains a problem.

Moses, at Yahweh's command, cut two tablets of stone and inscribed the "words of the covenant" upon them (34:1–28). The reason Moses must do this is to replace the tablets that he threw down and broke when he saw the people worshiping the golden calf in chapter 32. So the account in chapter 34 (esp. vv. 1–4) presupposes the story in chapter 32, and chapters 32—34 must be considered together, at least up to 34:29 (see n. 16).

As with Genesis 15 and Exodus 19—24, there are signs that Exodus 32—34 was dependent on Deuteronomy and the Deuteronomistic History and therefore cannot be considered the origin of the idea of the covenant between God and Israel.[17] One of the clearest signs of dependence is in Aaron's words to the people after he fashioned the golden calf: "These are your gods, O Israel, who brought you up from the land of Egypt" (32:4). This is a direct quote from 1 Kings 12:28. The dependence of the Exodus text on Kings, rather than the reverse, is evident in the use of the plural "gods," which makes sense in Kings, where Jeroboam erects two shrines with calves in Northern Israel, but not in Exodus, where Aaron molds only one calf.

Exodus 34:11–16 is especially marked with language and style drawn from Deuteronomy and the Deuteronomistic History.[18] The mandate to "observe what I command you today" (v. 11) occurs nearly word for word throughout Deuteronomy (4:40; 6:6; 7:11; etc.). In fact, the passage as a whole is very similar to Deuteronomy 7 with the list of Canaanite peoples (Exod. 34:11; Deut. 7:1), the warning not to make any covenant with them lest they become a "snare" (Exod. 34:12–16; Deut. 7:2–5, 16), and the command to destroy their cultic installations (Exod. 34:13; Deut. 7:5).[19]

All three of these passages—Genesis 15; Exodus 19—24; and Exodus 34—show influence from later biblical tradition, especially that of Deuteronomy and the Deuteronomistic History. None of the three, therefore, can be regarded as the beginning of the idea of a covenant between God and Israel. Obviously, Deuteronomy plays an important role in the development of that idea in the Bible, and we

---

[17]Cf. Perlitt, *Bundestheologie*, 203–32.

[18]Ibid., 220.

[19]In other respects Exodus 34:11–16 and the rest of Exodus 32—34 show influences from other writers or circles of tradition. For instance, 34:6–7 betrays similarities to Wisdom writings (Job, Proverbs, Ecclesiastes) as pointed out by Van Seters (*Life of Moses*, 246–48) following R. C. Dentan ("The Literary Affinities of Exodus 34:6f," *VT* 13 [1963]: 34–51). Thus, the author responsible for Exodus 32—34 may not have been simply a Deuteronomist, as Perlitt claimed, though this matter lies beyond our present concerns.

will explore this role in detail in the next chapter. First, however, we must examine one other possible source of the covenant idea—the eighth-century prophets and specifically Hosea.

Covenant in Hosea

The eighth-century prophets—Hosea, Amos, Isaiah, and Micah—represent a gap in the chronological presentation of covenant in the Bible. Scholars have long recognized that, with the possible exception of two verses in Hosea (6:7; 8:1), they do not refer to a covenant between God and Israel, despite the fact that such references would suit their purposes very well at points.[20] This situation is difficult to explain if the notion of the covenant was commonplace before and during the eighth century; it is understandable if the concept really developed thereafter.

The word "covenant" (*bᵉrît*) is used five times in the book of Hosea. Three of those occurrences refer to something other than the covenant between God and Israel.[21] The two references to covenant in Hosea 6:7 and 8:1 are more difficult to interpret. In 6:7 the kind of covenant is uncertain. Is it a covenant between God and Israel that has been broken, or one between humans? The Hebrew text of the verse literally reads,

> Like Adam they transgressed covenant
> There they broke faith with me.

At first glance this appears to allude to a covenant between God and Adam, presumably one that Adam broke when he ate of the forbidden fruit in the garden of Eden (Genesis 3). But modern scholars

---

[20]Scholars distinguish the original, eighth-century content of these books from later editorial layers. This is particularly important for Isaiah, whose chapters 40—55 and 56—66 are almost universally considered later works (called "Second" or Deutero-" Isaiah and "Third" or "Trito-" Isaiah, respectively) from the sixth and fifth centuries B.C.E. Only Isaiah 1—39 contains material from the eighth-century prophet Isaiah, and much of it is also later, including the mentions of the covenant in 24:5 and 33:8.

[21]In 2:18 (Heb. v. 20) the covenant is with the "beasts of the field, the birds of the air, and the creeping things of the grounds" (RSV) as an expression of fertility and harmony (*shālôm*) that will exist in the land in the future as a consequence of the reestablishment of the covenant between Yahweh and Israel that is characterized here in terms of a marriage. The reference in 10:4 has to do with covenants between humans and condemns the Israelites, probably their kings in particular (cf. James Luther Mays, *Hosea: A Commentary* [OTL; Philadelphia: Westminster Press, 1969], 138–41), for swearing false oaths when they make covenants. The covenant in 12:1 (Heb. v. 2) is an international treaty ("with Assyria") and therefore also has nothing to do with the covenant between God and Israel.

are nearly unanimous in rejecting this understanding. For one thing, there is no mention anywhere else in the Bible, including Genesis 2—3, of a covenant between God and Adam or Adam and Eve. Furthermore, the word "there" in the second line of the verse suggests that Adam may be a place name, and this possibility is strengthened by the places mentioned in subsequent verses—Gilead (v. 8) and Shechem (v. 9). A place named Adam is mentioned in Joshua 3:16 and is to be identified with a site (Tell ed-Damiye) in the territory of Gilead, east of the Jordan River. For these reasons, scholars typically read "in Adam" instead of "like Adam" at the beginning of verse 7 and take it as a geographical location.[22]

Unfortunately, recognizing Adam as a place name does not solve all the problems of the verse. In particular, it is still not clear what kind of covenant is envisaged here. The following verses describe crimes of violence on the part of priests. This would seem to favor the interpretation that the covenant here is the one between God and Israel, an interpretation reinforced by the observation that the verb "transgress" (Hebrew *'abar*) when used with "covenant" elsewhere in the Bible always refers to violating the covenant with God, not one with humans.[23] Still, Hosea 6:7 is unique among these passages in that its reference to covenant is indefinite. That is, it speaks not of transgressing *the* covenant or Yahweh's covenant, but simply "covenant" or "a covenant." The same is true of 10:4, which is often translated as plural, "covenants," referring to covenants between people (e.g., NRSV). In short, Hosea 6:7 seems to refer to some specific deed in the violent political chaos of the eighth century that we can no longer identify. It may have been a covenant among tribes or between Israel and another people, such as those described earlier in this chapter, to which Yahweh was a witness. But we cannot completely rule out the possibility that Hosea saw here a violation of the covenant between God and Israel.

The difficulty in 8:1 is not one of interpretation. "My covenant," which the people have "transgressed" (Hebrew *'abar*), clearly refers to the covenant between God and Israel. But the authenticity of this line has been called into question. Some scholars assert that verse 1b is a later addition, while others contend that the grounds for this

---

[22]This reading requires an emendation of the Hebrew preposition (*ke*) "like, as" to (*be*) "in." The two consonants look very much alike in some ancient scripts (ב and כ).

[23]See Nicholson, *God and His People*, 183–84.

assertion are not compelling.[24] Unfortunately, certainty on this matter is impossible. We are forced to say simply that Hosea probably did not invent the idea of covenant as an image for Yahweh's relationship to Israel. He may have been the first biblical writer to use this image, but this too is uncertain. In any case, it is clear that the covenant image was not central to his message but was only one image among many. The fact that he did not describe the covenant in detail or refer to it frequently throughout the book is significant and suggests that the idea was at most in its infancy.

We may summarize the results of this chapter by saying that the use of covenant imagery to describe the relationship between God and Israel was not current in Israel before the eighth century. The institution of covenant in the form of treaties binding clans, tribes, and nations together was very ancient. So it is certainly possible that the relationship between God and Israel was envisioned as a covenant long before the eighth century. But the use of this image in the Bible cannot be found with certainty before the eighth century. Even then it occurs only in the book of Hosea, twice, and both occurrences have been questioned. We must, therefore, look elsewhere for the origin of *the* covenant between God and Israel as it is presupposed by most biblical writers.

---

[24]Perlitt (*Bundestheologie*, 146–49) argues that 8:1b is a Deuteronomistic addition based on (1) the first person suffixes ("*my* covenant...*my* law"), which are atypical for Hosea but characteristic of Deuteronomy, and (2) the fact that other "calls to alarm" like the one in 8:1a (Hos. 5:8; Jer. 4:5; 6:1) are not followed by statements similar to the one in 8:1b. Nicholson (*God and His People*, 186–87) responds that these considerations are insufficient to indicate that 8:1b is secondary.

2

THE ORIGIN OF *THE* COVENANT IN ISRAEL

Covenant in Deuteronomy and the Deuteronomistic History

We saw in the last chapter that the origin of the covenant idea in ancient Israel is an open question. Whatever its origin, the image of covenant for God's relationship to Israel came to full expression relatively late in Israel's history in two works that are major components of the Hebrew Bible. They are known by scholars as the Deuteronomistic History and the priestly work, or P for short. They will furnish the topics of this chapter and the next.

The Deuteronomistic History

Deuteronomistic History is a term often used by biblical scholars to refer to the books of Deuteronomy plus Joshua, Judges,

1 and 2 Samuel, and 1 and 2 Kings.[1] It presupposes the belief that these books together originally comprised a unified work recounting the history of Israel from the time of Moses to the destruction of the kingdom of Judah in 586 B.C.E. (The division of this history into separate books took place much later. Also, the book of Ruth, found in English Bibles between Judges and 1 Samuel, is in a different location in the Hebrew Bible and was not part of the Deuteronomistic History.) This theory is based on the identification of several traits that the books share in common, especially the occurrence of a series of passages (mostly speeches) written in a common style and displaying a common theology. This style and theology are referred to as "Deuteronomistic" because they share the outlook of the book of Deuteronomy. These passages assess Israel's history according to the law set forth in Deuteronomy. Thus, the author(s)[2] of the Deuteronomistic History, often referred to simply as "Dtr," explains Israel's national successes and failures as the consequences of faithfulness or disobedience to the law, respectively. In particular, the destruction of the northern kingdom of Israel in 721 B.C.E. and the exile of Judah in 586 are seen as Yahweh's ultimate punishment for his people's continued sinfulness.

Contents of the Deuteronomistic History

Deuteronomy: Moses reviews the law for the people of
    Israel just before his death
Joshua: Israel under Joshua conquers and takes possession
    of the land of Canaan
Judges: Military leaders deliver the people from different
    foreign oppressors

---

[1]The term was coined by a German biblical scholar named Martin Noth in his famous book *Überlieferungsgeschichtliche Studien* (Halle: Max Niemeyer, 1943). This book is now available in an English translation as *The Deuteronomistic History* (JSOTSup 15; 2d ed.; Sheffield: Sheffield Academic Press, 1991).

[2]Scholars since Noth have disagreed about whether the Deuteronomistic History was written by a single author/editor or more than one. Also, while Noth dated the History to the exile, some scholars have argued for one or more preexilic versions. There have always been a few scholars who questioned the existence of the Deuteronomistic History as an original unit, but it has been and remains the consensus viewpoint. For reviews of scholarship on this questions see A. Graeme Auld, "The Former Prophets: Joshua, Judges, 1-2 Samuel, 1-2 Kings," in Steven L. McKenzie and M. Patrick Graham, eds., *The Hebrew Bible Today: An Introduction to Critical Issues* (Louisville, Ky.: Westminster John Knox Press, 1998), 53–68; and Steven L. McKenzie, "Deuteronomistic History," *ABD* 2:160–68.

1 Samuel 1—15: Samuel becomes Israel's last judge and
   anoints Saul as its first king
1 Samuel 16—2 Samuel 24: The rise and reign of David
1 Kings 1—11: David's death and the reign of Solomon
1 Kings 12—2 Kings 17: The division of the kingdom
   and a history of Israel and Judah to the fall of Israel
   (721 B.C.E.)
2 Kings 18—25: The history of Judah to its fall in 586
   B.C.E.

The impact of the Deuteronomistic History on the composition
and theology of the Bible as a whole was enormous. It was the springboard that gave rise to most of the rest of the Hebrew Bible and the
center from which the Bible's theology emanates. In the first place, it
occupies a large portion of the Bible, especially the Old Testament.
Also, it is the only real history of Israel included in the Bible.[3] Most
other books in the Bible either adapt Deuteronomistic theology or, in
a few cases, respond to it. This is certainly the case with regard to
covenant. Whether the concept arose from Hosea or elsewhere, the
author(s) of the Deuteronomistic History elaborated it into one of
the work's central doctrines. From there it became one of the principal teachings of the Bible. So the Deuteronomistic History must be
the starting point for our study of covenant.

The Book of the Covenant

The story of the Deuteronomistic History begins in 622 B.C.E.
with the finding of "the book of the law" in the temple during the
reign of King Josiah of Judah (2 Kgs. 22; cf. 2 Chr. 34). A corner-
stone of modern biblical scholarship is the identification of this law-
book in some form with Deuteronomy.[4] There are many reasons for

---

[3]The Tetrateuch tells the story of Israel up to Deuteronomy. It was put together, at least in
its present form, after the Deuteronomistic History. I will discuss portions of it below. The
books of 1 and 2 Chronicles overlap with the account of the monarchy in 2 Samuel—2 Kings.
It also was written after the Deuteronomistic History and used Samuel—Kings as its main
source, so it is not an independent history.

[4]This identification was an ancient one, but the first critical scholar to take it up was W.
M. L. de Wette in his important work, *Dissertatio critico-exegetica qua Deuteronomium a prioribus
Pentateuchi libris diversum, alius cuiusdam recentioris auctoris opus esse monstratur* (Jena, 1805).
For more detailed discussion of this identification see Moshe Weinfeld, *Deuteronomy 1—11: A
New Translation with Introduction and Commentary* (AB 5; New York: Doubleday, 1991), esp.
16–17, 81–84; and Weinfeld, "Deuteronomy, Book of," *ABD* 2:168–83.

this identification. Among the most significant for our present purposes are the following. The expression "the book of the law" (*sefer hattōrāh*), which describes Josiah's find (2 Kgs. 22:8, 11), is used in Deuteronomy for its contents (28:61; 29:21 [Heb. 29:20]; 30:10; 31:26) but does not occur elsewhere in the Pentateuch. "The book of the law" is also called "the book of the covenant" (2 Kgs. 23:2, 21), and when Josiah hears it read he leads the people in a covenant-renewal ceremony (23:3). This is consistent with Deuteronomy's self-portrait as "the words of the covenant" on the plains of Moab, in renewal of the covenant on Horeb (Deut. 5:2–3; 29:1 [Heb. 28:69]). In fact, the combination of expressions in 2 Kings 23:3—"commandments, testimonies, and statutes"—is peculiar to Deuteronomy. In addition, Josiah's consternation upon hearing the law book read (2 Kgs. 22:11–13) is best explained as a reaction to the curses in Deuteronomy 27—28, which, as we shall see, are an important indicator of the covenantal nature of the book.

The most important correlation between Deuteronomy and 2 Kings 23 is the fact that the religious reforms instituted by Josiah accord with the mandates of Deuteronomic law. By far the most significant of these—indeed the principle that lies at the heart of the reform movement—is centralization. This is the principle that the temple in Jerusalem is the only acceptable venue for worship. Josiah centralizes worship when he destroys the shrines to Yahweh throughout Judah and brings their priests up to Jerusalem (2 Kgs. 23:8–9). Centralization is an especially important ingredient of Deuteronomy's prescriptions for Passover (16:1–8), where it is expressly forbidden to offer the Passover sacrifice "within any of your towns" (16:5) but is commanded "at the place that Yahweh your God will choose" (16:2, 6). Second Kgs. 23:21–23 notes that Josiah kept the Passover *in Jerusalem* as mandated in the book of the covenant. The language of Josiah's decree ("make Passover to Yahweh your God," 2 Kgs. 23:21) even matches that of Deuteronomy's regulation ("you shall make Passover to Yahweh your God," Deut. 16:1). As the following chart shows, all the reforms carried out by Josiah in 2 Kings 23 according to the book of the law found earlier in 2 Kings 22 match Deuteronomy's regulations.[5]

---

[5]The chart is borrowed from Ernest W. Nicholson, *Deuteronomy and Tradition* (Philadelphia: Fortress Press, 1967), 3. Cf. Weinfeld, *Deuteronomy 1—11*, 16–17 and 81–82.

2 Kings 23	Deuteronomy
Abolition of the Asherim (vv. 4, 6, 7, 14)	7:5; 12:3; 16:21
The host of heaven (vv. 4, 5)	17:3
Destruction of the "pillars" (v. 14)	7:5; 12:3; etc.
Heathen high places (v. 13)	7:5; 12:2–3; etc.
Worship of sun and moon (vv. 5, 11)	17:3
Sacred prostitution (v. 7)	23:18
Molech cult (v. 10)	12:31; 18:10
Foreign gods (v. 13)	12; 13
Necromancy (v. 24)	18:11

"The book of the law" or "the book of the covenant" was probably actually written specifically for the seventh-century reform under Josiah, although it may contain older laws. The purported finding of a book that had been hidden or lost was a common strategy in the ancient world to justify important religious or social change, and in this case the book was found at an auspicious moment and supported precisely the measures that the reformers wished to implement.[6] The various laws in Deuteronomy, then, were collected into the "book of the law" under Josiah and presented in this new form and interpretation as support for his reform measures. This does not mean that Deuteronomy should be construed as a "pious fraud." Its authors were not seeking to deceive anyone but were trying to preserve a legacy that they sincerely believed had its origins with Moses. The seventh-century date for Deuteronomy is also indicated by its impact on the language and style of literature from the late seventh century on[7] and by features of the book that are due to direct influence from the Assyrian empire of the seventh century. Chief among the latter is the list of curses in Deuteronomy 28:27–35, which is dependent on the vassal treaties of the Assyrian king, Esarhaddon (ca. 672 B.C.E.). These treaties, in turn, helped to shape Deuteronomy's idea of covenant, as we will see below.

---

[6]As R. E. Clements (*Deuteronomy* [OTG; Sheffield: JSOT, 1989], 71) puts it: "It is far better to accept that its authors tried hard to preserve something in Israel's life that they felt to be indispensable and ancient, rather than that they were fortunate enough to find an ancient scroll which happened to suit their needs exactly!" On "book finding" in this story and the ancient world as a literary device see Thomas C. Römer, "Transformations in Deuteronomistic Biblical Historiography: On Book-Finding and Other Literary Strategies," *ZAW* 109 (1997): 1–11 and the other works he cites.

[7]Moshe Weinfeld, "Deuteronomy: The Present State of Inquiry," *JBL* 86 (1967): 250–51; and Weinfeld, "Deuteronomy," *ABD* 2:174.

Just who the individuals responsible for compiling the book of the law were is difficult to say. Second Kings 22 mentions priests, scribes, and prophets in the context of the discovery and interpretation of the book of the law, and the concerns of each of these groups, as well as the elders of Judah, may be seen in the themes and interests on display in Deuteronomy.[8] In fact, the original "book of the law" behind Deuteronomy may well have been written by some sort of coalition of priests, scribes and court officials, prophets, and popular leadership.[9] This would explain not only the elements of Deuteronomy shared by these various groups but also the far-reaching impact of Deuteronomy on different segments of Judahite society.

Contents of the Book of Deuteronomy

The book of Deuteronomy uses four headings to divide itself into four sections of uneven length. The four headings are:

"These are the words that Moses spoke to all Israel beyond Jordan in the wilderness…" (1:1)

"This is the law that Moses set before the children of Israel; these are the testimonies, the statutes, and the ordinances, that Moses spoke to the children of Israel when they came out of Egypt, on the other side of the Jordan…" (4:44–46a)

"These are the words of the covenant that Yahweh commanded Moses to make with the children of Israel in the land of Moab, besides the covenant he had made with them at Horeb." (28:69 [Eng. 29:1])

---

[8]Gerhard von Rad (*Deuteronomy: A Commentary* [OTL; Philadelphia: Westminster Press, 1966], 23–27; *Studies in Deuteronomy,* trans. D. M. Stalker [SBT; Chicago: Henry Regnery, 1953], esp. 60–70) saw the book as sermonic material from Levitical priests. Moshe Weinfeld (*Deuteronomy and the Deuteronomic School* [Oxford: Clarendon Press, 1972], 244–319; "Deuteronomy," *ABD*, 2:181–82) linked Deuteronomy with scribal circles responsible for education in the royal court and for producing Wisdom writings such as the book of Proverbs. Nicholson (*Deuteronomy and Tradition*) made a case for prophets being the authors of Deuteronomy. Leslie J. Hoppe ("The Origins of Deuteronomy," Ph.D. dissertation, Northwestern University, 1978) pointed to the prominence of the elders in Deuteronomy and suggested that they were behind its composition.

[9]Cf. Rainer Albertz, *A History of Israelite Religion in the Old Testament Period,* vol. 1, *From the Beginnings to the End of the Monarchy* (OTL; Louisville, Ky.: Westminster/John Knox Press, 1994), 201–6.

"This is the blessing with which Moses, the man of God, blessed the children of Israel before his death." (33:1)

Within the four sections marked off by these headings occur other divisions or subdivisions that are distinguishable from content.

1:1—4:43 This first section contains a historical review of Israel's journeys in the wilderness from Mount Horeb, where the law was given, to their current location opposite Baal-Peor on the eastern escarpment of the Jordan (1:1—3:29). This is followed by a sermon admonishing Israel to keep the law (4:1–40) and by the designation of three "cities of refuge" east of the Jordan (4:41–43).

4:44—28:68 The largest section, essentially chapters 5—28, falls into three portions. Chapters 5—11 (following an extension of the second heading in 4:44–49) are a discourse or series of discourses by Moses on the importance of faithfulness to Yahweh and his commandments. They include Deuteronomy's version of the Ten Commandments (5:6–21), the *Shema* (6:4), with its confession that Israel's God, Yahweh, is one, ordinances about holy war and against making any alliances with the peoples in the promised land because Israel is Yahweh's elect (chapter 7), and the episode of the calf fashioned by the people while Moses was on the mountain (9:8—10:11). This subsection ends with the instructions regarding the ceremony to take place on Mounts Ebal and Gerizim in the promised land, where the people are to recite the blessings for obedience and the curses for disobedience of the law (11:26–32). Chapters 12—26 then give the law code proper. Although "law" is the conventional term for this material, it is something of a misnomer. Many of these laws are closely paralleled by those in other ancient Near Eastern codes, like the Code of Hammurabi. But the homiletic tone and focus on religious matters in Deuteronomy are very different from such codes. A more accurate term for the biblical "law" would be "instruction," which is the real meaning of the Hebrew word *tôrāh*. The "law" is followed by the blessings and (especially) the curses (chapters 27—28) to be recited on Mounts Ebal and Gerizim.

29—32 The next section, essentially chapters 29—30, constitute another speech by Moses; this time the setting is a covenant-making ceremony on the Moabite plain. The speech reflects on the blessings and curses of the previous two chapters, encouraging obedience and warning about the consequences of disobedience based on past experiences. Chapter 31 describes Moses' farewell to the people

(vv. 1–6) and his commissioning of Joshua (vv. 7–8, 14–15, 23), interrupted by his writing and preservation of the law (vv. 9–13, 24–29) and a long introduction from Yahweh to the song in the next chapter (vv. 16–22). Chapter 32 is the Song of Moses (vv. 1–43) followed by an epilogue (vv. 44–47) and Yahweh's instructions for Moses to ascend Mount Nebo to die (vv. 48–52).

33—34 The final two chapters contain the Blessing of Moses (33), another poetic piece, and an account of Moses' death and the transfer of leadership to Joshua (34).

The most influential proposal regarding the organizational principle underlying Deuteronomy's structure holds that it follows the outline of ancient Near Eastern treaties.[10] There are six elements typically present in such treaties: (1) a preamble, which identified the suzerain or overlord by titles and ancestry; (2) a historical prologue, which described the past relationship between suzerain and vassal, emphasizing the suzerain's beneficence; (3) the stipulations assumed by both parties, but especially the obligations of the vassal toward the suzerain; (4) provision for the deposit—usually in the temple of the vassal's deity—and periodic reading of the treaty document; (5) a list of gods as witnesses, by whom both parties, but especially the vassal, swore allegiance to the treaty; (6) the list of curses and blessings accruing to the vassal for success or failure in complying with the treaty's stipulations.

According to this proposal, Yahweh was cast in the role of the suzerain and Israel in that of the vassal. The six elements of the treaty form appeared in Deuteronomy as follows:[11] (1) Deuteronomy 4:44–49 fulfilled the function of the preamble; (2) chapters 5—11 were the "historical-parenetic prologue"; (3) 12:1—26:15 represented the stipulations; (4) provisions for depositing and periodic reading may

---

[10]George E. Mendenhall ("Covenant Forms in Israelite Tradition," *BA* 17 [1954]: 49–76) initially applied the treaty form to the entire Pentateuch or Torah, arguing that the Decalogue contained the treaty stipulations and was preceded by a historical prologue and that the other treaty elements were preserved elsewhere in the Torah. His proposal was refined by Dennis J. McCarthy (*Treaty and Covenant: A Study in Form in the Ancient Oriental Documents and in the Old Testament* [AnBib 21; Rome: Pontifical Biblical Institute, 1963; 2d ed.; AnBib 21A; 1978], references here are to the second edition), who applied it specifically to Deuteronomy. For more details see Nicholson, *God and His People*, 56–82. For an accessible presentation of this topic see Delbert R. Hillers, *Covenant: The History of a Biblical Idea* (Seminars in the History of Ideas; Baltimore/London: Johns Hopkins Press, 1969).

[11]This is essentially McCarthy's list (*Treaty and Covenant*, 186) supplemented in items 4 and 5 with observations of other scholars.

be found in 10:1–5; 31:9–13, 24–26; (5) there is no mention, of course, of other gods as witnesses, but heaven and earth are invoked instead (4:26; 30:19; 31:28), and oaths are taken before them (29:10–29 [Heb. 9–28]) 26:16-19; and (6) 28:1–68 contains the blessings and curses.

The final item in this list, the curses for violating the covenant/treaty, is of particular importance. The basic treaty form outlined above was adapted by different cultures in the ancient Near East for nearly two thousand years.[12] But the best examples are those from the Hittites in the fourteenth century and the Assyrians in the eighth and seventh centuries B.C.E. One of the differences between the two is that the Assyrian exemplars contain much longer lists of curses than do the Hittite versions. Deuteronomy, with its extensive set of curses in chapter 28, has more in common with the later, Assyrian treaties than with the Hittite ones. Indeed, Deuteronomy's is by far the most extensive set of curses of this type that we have from the ancient Near East. The similarity between curses in Deuteronomy and in the vassal treaties of Esarhaddon (ca. 672 B.C.E.) is especially striking, as the following comparison drawn by Weinfeld shows.[13]

Deut. 28:27: The Lord will smite you with Egyptian inflammation…and with scars from which you shall never recover.	Vassal Treaty of Esarhaddon (VTE) 419–20: May Sin…the light of heaven and earth clothe you with leprosy; may he not order your entering into the presence of the gods or king.

---

[12]See McCarthy's survey of ancient Near Eastern treaties in part 1 of *Treaty and Covenant,* and especially his chapter 7, "The Treaties: a Basic Unity."

[13]Weinfeld, *Deuteronomy and the Deuteronomic School,* 117–27. The initial publication of the Esarhaddon treaties was D. J. Wiseman, "The Vassal Treaties of Esarhaddon," *Iraq* 20 (1958): 1–99. Weinfeld also pointed out other isolated, striking parallels between Deuteronomy 28 and the Assyrian vassal treaties (VTE):

Deut. 28:23 (RSV): And the heavens over your head shall be brass, and the earth under you shall be iron.	VTE 448–50: A mother [will lock her door] against her daughter. In your hunger eat the flesh of your sons! In the famine and want may one man eat the flesh of another.
Deut. 28:53–57 (RSV): And you shall eat the offspring of your own body, the flesh of your sons and daughters…in the siege and in the distress…The most tender…woman will grudge…to her son and to her daughter…she will eat them secretly, for want of all things…in the siege and in the distress.	VTE 528–31: May they [the gods] make your ground like iron so that no one can plough [cut] it. Just as rain does not fall from a brazen heaven, so may rain and dew not come upon your fields and pastures.

Deut. 28:28–29: The Lord will smite you with madness and blindness and confusion of mind, and you shall grope at noonday as the blind gropes in the darkness, and you shall not prosper in your ways, and you shall only be oppressed and robbed continually, and there shall be none to help you.

VTE 422–24: May Shamash…not render you a just judgement [not give you a reliable decision]; may he deprive you of the sight of your eyes [so that] they will wander about in darkness.

Deut. 28:26: Your corpses shall be food for all birds of the heaven and for beasts of the earth.

VTE 425–27: May Ninurta…fell you with his swift arrow; may he fill the steppe with your corpses; may he feed your flesh to the vulture [and] the jackal.

Deut. 28:30a: You shall betroth a wife, and another man shall lie with her.

VTE 428–29: May Venus, the brightest of stars, make your wives lie in your enemy's lap while your eyes look [at them].

Deut. 28:30b: You shall build a house, and you shall not dwell in it. V. 32: Your sons and your daughters shall be given to another people.

VTE 429–30a: May your sons not be masters of your house.

Deut. 28:33: A nation which you have not known shall eat up the fruit of your ground and of your labors…

VTE 430b: May a foreign enemy divide all your goods.

In addition to the obvious similarities of ideas and language, Weinfeld noted that the order of curses in the two documents was nearly identical and that the association of skin disease with judicial blindness in Deuteronomy 28:27–29 made sense only in the light of Mesopotamian religion. While the threats they describe—drought and famine, disease and plague, siege, warfare, and exile—represent the fears and experiences common for the day, these similarities are strong indications of direct borrowing.

Despite these similarities, it is evident that the book of Deuteronomy per se is not a covenant or treaty document. There are important differences between Deuteronomy as it now stands and the ancient Near Eastern treaties.[14] Deuteronomy does not present itself as a treaty but as a valedictory speech by Moses. Nor does it refer to

---

[14]See Nicholson, *God and His People,* esp. 70–78; and A. D. H. Mayes, *Deuteronomy* (NCB; Greenwood, S.C.: Attic, 1979), 30–34.

Yahweh as king (suzerain).[15] Elements 4 (provisions for treaty documents) and 5 (invocation of witnesses) of the treaty form are scattered throughout Deuteronomy rather than occurring in the normal treaty sequence.[16] Most important, it contains numerous features that cannot be incorporated in a treaty form or go far beyond it. These include not only the final three chapters of the book, Song of Moses, Blessing of Moses, and account of Moses' death, but also the lengthy historical prologue in Deuteronomy 1—4, which is unmatched in the treaties, as is the scope and parenetic nature of the "stipulations" in Deuteronomy's law code. Even the closest parallel between Deuteronomy and the treaties, the curses in chapter 28, is not exact. It includes blessings, which do not appear in the Assyrian treaties, and also betrays the work of more than one writer.[17]

Nevertheless, the similarities demonstrate the familiarity of the writers of Deuteronomy with Assyrian treaties. It is likely that this treaty relationship was the source for Deuteronomy's image of a covenant between God and Israel. Assuming this was the case, we can learn a good deal about the biblical covenant by examining it with the qualities of the ancient Near Eastern treaty in mind. It may even be that the original Deuteronomy—the "book of the law" or "book of the covenant"—was in the form of a treaty document. Unfortunately, this original book cannot be recovered because it has been revised and expanded by Dtr. But we may use this fact to our advantage. Since it is difficult, if not impossible, to determine what portions of Deuteronomy belonged to the original book and what came from later editors,[18] we may extend our field of vision to include the entire Deuteronomistic History and thereby gather more information about the basic understanding of covenant in the Bible.

---

[15]Except for Deuteronomy 33:5, which is part of a later addition to the book and whose meaning is disputed.

[16]McCarthy (*Treaty and Covenant*, 188–205) contended that the two passages framing this central discourse in Deuteronomy 4:1–40 and 28:69—30:20 were miniatures of the covenant form and that they were by a later writer. Hence, the instances of elements 4 and 5 that fall within these passages should not count as part of the main treaty of Deuteronomy.

[17]Deuteronomy 28:48–68 is usually seen as a later addition. Cf. Nicholson, *God and His People*, 75–77.

[18]Scholars generally agree in seeing chaps. 1—4 and 29—34 as later framing additions to the original level of Deuteronomy. The majority of references to covenant in the book occur within these framing passages. How much of the material remaining in the kernel (chaps. 5—28) was part of the original book is hard to say, though scholars have assigned significant portions of it also to later editing. For a recent overview of these literary matters see Thomas C. Römer, "The Book of Deuteronomy," in Steven L. McKenzie and M. Patrick Graham, eds., *The History of Israel's Traditions: The Heritage of Martin Noth* (JSOTSup 182; Sheffield: Sheffield Academic Press, 1994), 178–212.

As with most treaties, it is the suzerain, Yahweh, who takes the initiative in establishing the covenant. The covenant presupposes a historical relationship between the two parties. (This is true whether or not Deuteronomy 5—11 actually fulfills the role of the historical prologue of a treaty.) The difference is that unlike the treaty, which is typically based on the overlord's *conquest* of the vassal, the covenant is grounded in Yahweh's *rescue* of Israel from an oppressive overlord, the pharaoh of Egypt (Deut. 7:6–8). The covenant, therefore, is an act of grace, sealing Israel's election as Yahweh's people: "The LORD your God has chosen you out of all the peoples on earth to be his people, his treasured possession" (7:6, NRSV).

In Deuteronomy the covenant itself, in a sense, is part of the history of God's relationship with Israel. Just as Deuteronomy is "second law," the covenant it describes is the second covenant. Yahweh made the original covenant with Israel at the sacred mountain of Horeb (called Sinai elsewhere in the Pentateuch) when he brought them out of Egypt (5:2). This covenant was initially with the exodus generation, and it is that generation rather than the patriarchs (Abraham, Isaac, Jacob) that is meant when Deuteronomy refers to "your ancestors" (lit. "fathers").[19] In Deuteronomy, Moses addresses the next generation as they are ready to enter the land of Canaan. Most of them were not alive at the time of the original covenant. Yet Moses tells them that the covenant is with them (5:3; 29:1 [Heb. 28:69]). They are part of Yahweh's elect people, Israel. Hence, this covenant is not a new covenant but a renewal of the one with their forebears in the exodus generation.

The same idea of the inheritance of the covenant is what makes it still valid for the even later generation at the time of Josiah.[20] Since

---

[19]Thomas C. Römer (*Israels Väter: Untersuchungen zur Väterthematik im Deuteronomium und in der deuteronomistischen Tradition* [OBO 99; Freiburg/Göttingen: Universitätsverlag/ Vandenhoeck & Ruprecht, 1990]) has shown that the references to the patriarchs by name in Deuteronomy (e.g., in 6:10) were added later, presumably after it was combined with the stories about the patriarchs in the Tetrateuch.

[20]The Deuteronomistic History as it now stands describes two other covenants between God and Israel. The one made by Joshua (Josh. 24:25) is probably a later addition that was not originally a part of the History. (Cf. Richard D. Nelson, *Joshua: A Commentary* [OTL; Louisville, Ky.: Westminster John Knox Press, 1997], 265–70.) The one at the time of Joash (2 Kgs. 11:17) takes place in the context of a royal overthrow and involves three parties—the new king in addition to Yahweh and the people—so that it is of a different nature than the Horeb covenant. However, to the extent that it includes the people's pledge of loyalty to Yahweh alone (cf. v. 18) it should be viewed as a renewal of the covenant under Moses. The fact that Josiah carries out the only other clear renewal of the Horeb covenant is yet another connection of Josiah's "book of the covenant" with Deuteronomy.

Deuteronomy was actually written under Josiah, one of the authors' main points is that the covenant applies to their own contemporary audience. Thus, the covenant into which the people enter in 2 Kings 23:1–3 is not a new covenant but a renewal of the covenant of their ancestors described in Deuteronomy, which is itself a renewal of the original covenant at Horeb. And the covenant will continue beyond Josiah. That is why teaching the commandments to children is so important (6:7)—because it ensures the continuation of the covenant relationship with Yahweh. It is also why the "book of the covenant" is so important in the Deuteronomistic History. The stone tablets upon which the covenant was written did not exist in the seventh century when Deuteronomy was written; nor did the ark of the covenant that once housed those tablets. The book of the covenant served as a replacement for those tablets so that the covenant with God could remain intact.

The covenantal relationship is best described as "divine commitment and human obligation."[21] This description captures both the two-sided nature of the covenantal relationship and the fact that in Deuteronomy the real onus for keeping the covenant is on Israel. Like the suzerain, Yahweh makes a commitment to Israel, promising to protect and bless them if they remain loyal to him. Yahweh committed himself by swearing an oath to the ancestors ("fathers") of the present generation to give them the land (6:23). The fact that the people of Israel now stand perched on the plain of Moab ready to enter Canaan shows that Yahweh is faithful to his commitment: "Know therefore that the LORD your God is God, the faithful God who maintains covenant loyalty with those who love him and keep his commandments, to a thousand generations" (7:9, NRSV). He brought them out of Egypt and through the wilderness in accordance with his promise (8:14–16). He will now defeat the inhabitants of Canaan and deliver the land to Israel if they will but trust him and obey the law (7:16–26; 9:1–12; 11:22–25).

Israel's success or failure turns on the fulfillment of their obligation to the covenantal terms. The original covenant at Horeb consisted of the Ten Commandments (5:1–21; cf. 4:13); but in the form being renewed in Deuteronomy, it includes the law code in chapters 12—26. Israel's covenantal obligation, therefore, may be summed up in a

---

[21]Borrowing the title of an article by David Noel Freedman, "Divine Commitment and Human Obligation: The Covenant Theme," *Interp* 18 (1964): 419–31.

single word: obedience. Yahweh's faithfulness to his covenantal promises toward those who obey and hence "love" him is matched by his
vengefulness against the disobedient who "hate" him. The statement
quoted above from 7:9 continues in verse 10: "and who repays in
their own person those who reject him. He does not delay but repays
in their own person those who reject him."

The word that the NRSV translates "reject" is actually the Hebrew word for "hate." "Love" and "hate" are treaty terms. The vassal
who observes the stipulations of the treaty and remains loyal to his
suzerain is said to "love" him; the one who breaks the treaty "hates"
his overlord. Similarly, those who obey the laws in the covenant with
Yahweh love him; those who disobey hate him. The primary test of
covenantal faithfulness is exclusive worship of Yahweh. Apostasy is
such a danger that anyone guilty of breaking the covenant by worshiping other gods must immediately be purged from Israel (17:2–7).
This is also the reason for the harsh measures prescribed against the
Canaanites (7:1–5; 12:29–31).

The incentive for obedience to the covenantal stipulations is the
alternatives of reward/punishment, or in treaty language, blessing and
curse. Punishment for disobedience is threatened immediately upon
the transgressor (7:10) and upon that person's descendants for generations to come (5:9). We have already seen that curses from Assyrian
treaties are borrowed directly into Deuteronomy. But unlike those
treaties, Deuteronomy also lists substantial blessings to accrue to the
faithful (28:1–14). Both their land and progeny will be blessed prac-
tically forever, that is, to a thousand generations (7:9, 12–16).

The rest of the Deuteronomistic History attests to Yahweh's pa-
tience with Israel. It is only after centuries of repeated covenant breaking that destruction comes to Israel (2 Kgs. 17, esp. vv. 15, 35, 38).
Judah lasts another 135 years before its capture by the Babylonians.
To be sure, these events are strikingly like the curses for covenantal
violation in Deuteronomy. Yet, even so, the Deuteronomistic History never says that the covenant has been completely abrogated. To
the contrary, the covenant seems to become grounds for hope. Second Kings 13:23, a late addition to the Deuteronomistic History,
sees the covenant with Abraham, Isaac, and Jacob as the reason that
Yahweh had not as yet destroyed all of his people. If we look for a
moment beyond the History to the book of Ezra, which was written
at least a century later, we find Ezra calling for a covenant with God

to put away non-Jewish wives and children (10:3). Since this call is based on an interpretation of the law in Deuteronomy 7:3–4, the covenant should be understood as yet another renewal of the Horeb covenant, which Ezra sees as still in effect after the exile.

In sum, our survey of covenant in Deuteronomy and the Deuteronomistic History, with its background in ancient Near Eastern treaties, has revealed several features of covenant that will prove to be important in future discussion. God's covenant with Israel originates with the exodus generation. But it is not for that generation alone. The same covenant is renewed by Moses with the next generation on the plains of Moab at the entrance to the promised land. The covenant is mutual to the extent that Yahweh commits himself to act on Israel's behalf as long as they obey the stipulations of the law incorporated into the covenant. He has already demonstrated his faithfulness to his commitments by bringing the Israelites out of Egyptian bondage and through the wilderness to the promised land. He promises future prosperity and blessing in the land. The language of the covenant is the language of treaty, in the terms *blessing* and *curse*, as well as in the use of the words *love* and *hate*. These words give rise to a theology of covenant that involves the idea of retribution, of reward and punishment, according to which good deeds and righteous living are rewarded, and wickedness is punished. We will explore these and other theological implications of covenant in the final chapter of this book.

3

FROM CREATION TO SINAI
Covenant in the Priestly Writings

The priestly writings, designated "P," refer to one of the authors or sources that some scholars postulate as responsible for the composition of the Pentateuch or Torah, the first five books of the Bible.[1] P stands for "priest," because they find evidence of priestly concerns in this strand of material and believe that it was written by one or more priests.

---

[1]On the documentary hypothesis see Viviano, "Source Criticism," in McKenzie and Haynes, eds., *To Each Its Own Meaning*, 35–57; and Van Seters, "The Pentateuch," in McKenzie and Graham, eds., *The Hebrew Bible Today*, 3–49. In its classical form the documentary hypothesis postulates four sources behind the Pentateuch, abbreviated as J, E, P, and D. J and E stand for "Jahwist" (Yahwist) and "Elohist" because of the names they favor for God ("Yahweh" and "Elohim," respectively). D stands for Deuteronomist. The book of Deuteronomy, as we have seen, is also part of the Deuteronomistic History and does not contain J, E, or P material. Scholars refer both to a Pentateuch and to a Tetrateuch, depending on whether Deuteronomy is included.

41

The clearest example of P material is in Genesis 1. It was in the beginning chapters of Genesis that careful readers first noticed the traces of different writers.[2] The order of creation in Genesis 1 is entirely different from that in Genesis 2, as the following chart shows.

Genesis 1	Genesis 2
light, day and night (vv. 1–5)	a man (v. 7)
sky (dome) and seas (vv. 6–8)	a garden (v. 8)
dry land, vegetation (vv. 9–13)	trees in the garden (v. 9)
sun, moon, stars (vv. 14–19)	land animals, birds (vv. 18–20)
birds, fish (vv. 20–23)	a woman (vv. 21–23)
land animals, humans (vv. 24–31)	

In Genesis 1 humans are the last item of creation, while in Genesis 2 the man is the first. In Genesis 1 men and women are created together, and there is no indication that only one pair is created as in Genesis 2. In Genesis 1 all the animals are created before people, but in Genesis 2 the animals are created after the man in an effort to find a companion for him, a process that eventually leads to the creation of the woman. Genesis 2 is a story, which continues into chapter 3; it has a plot and character development. Genesis 1 is a kind of elaborated list. It is apparent that two versions of creation have been set side by side in Genesis 1—2. It may well be that the story in chapter 2 was intended to be read as an elaboration of the creation of humans at the end of chapter 1. But the differences between them make clear that they were originally distinct.

The account in Genesis 1 extends beyond that chapter to include the first three verses of chapter 2. This is indicated by two considerations. First, the account in Genesis 1 is organized by days with creation taking place on six consecutive days. The same scheme then continues in 2:1–3 when God rests on the seventh day, so that the entire process occupies one week. Second, each version of creation begins with a similar formula. Again, the chart illustrates.

---

[2]Viviano sketches the history of the documentary hypothesis in her article on "Source Criticism," cited in n. 1.

Construction	Genesis 1:1–3	Genesis 2:4b–7
protasis ("when" clause)	When God began to create³ the heavens and the earth	When⁴ Yahweh God made earth and heavens
parenthetical clause	(the earth being formless and empty with darkness on the surface of the deep and a divine wind sweeping over the surface of the water)⁵	(no plant or herb of the field having yet sprung up on the earth, since Yahweh God had not caused it to rain on the earth and there was no human to work the ground, but a stream came up from the earth and watered the ground)
apodosis ("then" clause)	then God said, "Let there be light," and there was light.	then Yahweh God formed the man of dust from the ground and breathed into his nostrils the breath of life so that the man became a living being.

Creation accounts from the ancient Near East, especially Mesopotamia, often begin with temporal clauses.⁶ The fact that Genesis 2:4b–7 begins with a temporal clause and is the same syntactically as 1:1 marks it as the beginning of another creation account.

Each day's creation in Genesis 1 follows a pattern using stereotyped expressions in a fairly consistent sequence:

---

³The first verse of the Bible is grammatically impossible. Literally it reads, "In the beginning of God created the heavens and the earth." Translators must make one of two changes in the Hebrew vowels in order to render either "In the beginning, God created…" or "In the beginning of God's creating…," that is, "When God began to create…" The latter, though less common, is more likely because of parallels from other creation stories, as explained below. The NRSV translation, "In the beginning when God created…," is a conflation of these two possibilities and is grammatically indefensible.

⁴Literally "in the day that"—an idiom for "when."

⁵"Divine wind" is sometimes translated "the spirit of God," but it probably means an extremely powerful wind rather than God's spirit or a "wind from God" (NRSV).

⁶A good example outside of the Bible is the Babylonian creation story. Its title, "Enuma Elish," is the first two words of the story, which form a temporal clause meaning "When on high…"

And God said, "Let there be X"
And it was so
God called
And God saw that it was good
And there was evening and there was morning the Y day[7]

There are two days (3 and 6) in which this pattern is repeated, thus recounting the creation of two distinct categories of things. Verses 9–10 read: "And God said, 'Let the waters under the sky be gathered together into one place, and let the dry land appear.' And it was so. God called the dry land Earth, and the waters that were gathered together he called Seas. And God saw that it was good." At this point we expect to read, "And there was evening and there was morning the third day." Instead, the creation formula begins again: "And God said, 'Let the earth put forth vegetation'…And it was so [v. 11]…God saw that it was good" (v. 12). Then, "And there was evening and there was morning, the third day." Similarly, in verses 24–25, "And God said, 'Let the earth bring forth living creatures of every kind'…And it was so…And God saw that it was good." Once again, we expect "And there was morning and there was evening the sixth day." Instead the pattern starts over. "And God said, 'Let us make humankind' [v. 26] …And it was so [v. 30]. God saw everything that he had made, and indeed, it was very good." Then, "And there was evening and there was morning, the sixth day" (v. 31).

In short, it looks like a creation account in eight installments has been compressed into six days:

day 1: light   day 4: sun, moon, stars
day 2: sky   day 5: birds, fish
day 3: seas and dry land,   day 6: land animals,
vegetation   humans
            day 7: Sabbath

This is a meticulously balanced and organized account. There is "vertical" balance, as there is one item or category of items created on days 1–2 and 4–5 and two such items or categories created on days 3 and 6. There is also "horizontal" balance between days 1 and 4, 2 and

---

[7]The expression "evening and morning" instead of "morning and evening," as we would say it, occurs because in the Jewish calendar the next day begins at sunset. This also illustrates the culturally determined nature of the document in Genesis 1.

5, and 3 and 6. The light created on day 1 matches the bodies of light—sun, moon, and stars—created on day 4. On day 2 the dome of the sky is created and the waters above the dome separated from those beneath it; this corresponds to day 5 when the residents of sky and water, birds and fish, are created. Then the creation of dry land and vegetation on day 3 is matched by the creation of animals and humans, who live on the land and consume the vegetation, on day 6.

The reason for the compression of creation from eight install-ments into six days was to reserve the seventh day for God to rest and thereby to institute the Sabbath. This is an extremely powerful theo-logical grounding for Sabbath observation. The institution of the Sab-bath is established at the very origin of the world and is therefore fundamental to the cosmos. If God kept the Sabbath, how could hu-mans fail to do so?

The concern for keeping the Sabbath is one of the features that betrays the priestly origin and orientation of Genesis 1:1—2:3. The priests were the guardians of the Sabbath and similar institutions as-sociated with the religious (especially ritual) life of ancient Israel. The priestly perspective was not the only possible one, as is evident from the different versions of the Ten Commandments in Exodus 20 and Deuteronomy 5. Both include a command to keep the Sabbath, but the reason for doing so varies. Exodus 20:8–11 is the P version. Like P's creation account, it locates the reason for Sabbath observation in creation: "For in six days Yahweh made heaven and earth…but rested on the seventh day; therefore Yahweh blessed the sabbath day and consecrated it" (v. 11). But the reason in Deuteronomy 5:12–15 is entirely different. There the Sabbath has the social function of afford-ing rest to one's animals and slaves, and the Israelite is to "remember that you were a slave in the land of Egypt" (v. 15) so as not to oppress his workers.

These features of Genesis 1:1—2:3 reflect qualities typical of P's work in general. They exemplify an interest in matters of ritual and law. As we will see, virtually all of the law of Moses in the Tetrateuch is assigned by scholars to P. Genesis 1:1—2:3 also contains a number of words that are typical of P's vocabulary. Among those that will prove most significant for our study of covenant are the name P uses for God—*'elōhîm* rather than Yahweh—and the blessing formula "Be fruitful and multiply." In addition, the features of this text show P's organizational skill and concern for order and detail. P's organizational skills and techniques are especially important because he was the editor of the Pentateuch.[8] He used several devices to structure the Pentateuchal material. One such device in Genesis was the expression "these are the generations of" (or in one case "the book of the generations of") that occurs as a heading at ten points throughout Genesis:

2:4a. These are the generations of the heavens and the earth
5:1. This is the book of the generations of Adam
6:9. These are the generations of Noah
10:1. These are the generations of the sons of Noah
11:10. These are the generations of Shem
11:27. These are the generations of Terah
25:12. These are the generations of Ishmael
25:19. These are the generations of Isaac
36:1. These are the generations of Esau
37:2. These are the generations of Jacob

In each case the statement *introduces* material about the descendants of the person or thing named. Thus, 37:2 introduces stories about Jacob's sons, especially Joseph; 36:1 introduces genealogical material about Esau; 25:19 introduces the story of Isaac's sons, Jacob and Esau; and so on. Slight variations are 6:9, which introduces the flood story, and 2:4a, which introduces the story of Adam and Eve. But in every case the P "generations" statement is still a heading to mostly non-P material and is, therefore, editorial.

The System of Covenants in P

The main, overarching editorial device used by P in the Pentateuch is his system of covenants. P divided the account of history from creation to Moses into four epochs by means of a series of three covenants with Noah, Abraham, and Moses. This has long been recognized. Indeed, Julius Wellhausen, the German scholar responsible for giving the documentary hypothesis its classic formulation, referred to P as *liber quattuor foederum* ("Q" for short), the "book of four covenants."[9] Wellhausen included a covenant with Adam as the first of the four covenants. But as we have seen, there is no explicit reference

---

[8]As demonstrated by Frank Moore Cross, *Canaanite Myth and Hebrew Epic: Essays in the History of the Religion of Israel* (Cambridge, Mass.: Harvard University Press, 1973), 301–21.

[9]Julius Wellhausen, *Prolegomena to the History of Ancient Israel* (Gloucester, Mass.: Peter Smith, 1957), 8, n. 2.

to a covenant with Adam or Eve. The word *covenant* does not occur at all in Genesis until the Noah story. In addition, as shown above, the story of Adam and Eve in Genesis 2—3 is not P anyway.

Although Genesis 1:1—2:3 does not mention covenant, it does prepare the reader for the series of covenants to come. It does this in two ways. First, it articulates the blessing, "Be fruitful and multiply," that will accompany each of the three covenants in some form. Second, as we have seen, it describes the origin of Sabbath, which will serve as the sign of the covenant in which P is most interested, namely the one under Moses at Sinai (Exod. 31:12–17).

The three covenants that P relates follow a specific format, each with an accompanying law, sign, and blessing.

Covenant	Law	Sign	Blessing
Noah	blood	rainbow	Be fruitful and multiply.
Abraham	circumcision	circumcision	I will make you fruitful; I will make nations of you.
Israel at Sinai	the law of Moses	Sabbath	I will make you fruitful and multiply you.

The covenant with Noah (Gen. 9) is established after the flood. It is a universal covenant made with Noah, his sons, their descendants, and all the animals who survived the flood with them (9:9–10). God makes a commitment never again to destroy the world with a flood: "I establish my covenant with you, that never again shall all flesh be cut off by the waters of a flood, and never again shall there be a flood to destroy the earth" (9:11, NRSV). As a sign of this commitment, God gives the rainbow: "I have set my bow in the clouds, and it shall be a sign of the covenant between me and the earth" (9:13, NRSV). God blesses Noah and his sons with the same blessing found in P's creation account: "Be fruitful and multiply" (9:1, 7, NRSV). God also imposes an obligation or law of the covenant. Humans (and animals) have been vegetarians. God now allows them to eat meat (9:3), with the stipulation, "You shall not eat flesh with its life, that is, its blood" (9:4, NRSV). Another dimension of this law is the prohibition against bloodshed (murder): "Whoever sheds the blood of a human, by a human shall that person's blood be shed; for in his own image God made humankind" (9:6, NRSV). The language of this last statement is again taken from P's creation account where "God created humankind in his image" (1:27).

In P's scheme, the covenant with Noah remains in effect even after the other covenants with Abraham and Moses are instituted. The Noah covenant is with all people; the ones with Abraham and Moses are more limited and apply only to Israelites or Jews. But the latter two covenants do not replace the one with Noah. God's promise not to destroy the world with flood still stands, and the rainbow still attests to it. Similarly, the law of blood still applies to all people, Jews included. An illustration of this is found in the story of the early church in Acts 15. When the "apostles and elders" of the Jerusalem church determined that God had accepted uncircumcised Gentiles into the church, they wrote to the Gentile Christians in Asia Minor in an effort to reassure them. In their letter they asked the Gentiles to refrain from certain practices that were offensive to Jews. One of these was "blood" (15:20, 29), which probably refers to the eating of blood.[10] The Jewish Christians understood the covenant with Noah still to be in effect, despite the covenants with Abraham, Moses, and even Christianity, and to apply to Gentiles as well as Jews.

P's version of the covenant with Abraham is found in Genesis 17. Here God reveals himself with a new name—*El Shadday*, often translated "God Almighty" (NRSV), and this becomes a favorite epithet for God in P. God also changes Abraham's name in this chapter from Abram (ostensibly "exalted father") to Abraham (ostensibly "father of a multitude").[11] The name change is indicative of God's covenant with Abraham. God blesses Abraham by promising to make nations of his descendants and to give the land of Canaan to his offspring (17:6–8). In addition to the blessing of the covenant, there is also a sign and a law of the covenant. In this case they are the same—circumcision. "This is my covenant, which you shall keep, between me and you and your offspring after you: Every male among you shall be

---

[10]In both verses 20 and 29 the additional phrase "and from what is strangled" appears. This is likely a gloss trying to explain what is meant by "blood." An animal that was killed by strangling would not have the blood drained out of it and would have been considered unfit for eating, according to P's law.

[11]I say "ostensibly" because the two forms are actually linguistic variants of the same name, and there is no difference in meaning between them.

circumcised" (17:10, NRSV). Abraham and his descendants, therefore, are obligated to keep the rite of circumcision. Then, in the next
verse, circumcision is explicitly called a sign of the covenant. The
covenant with Abraham is also explicitly designated an "eternal" covenant (17:7, 13). It is understood to continue in effect even after the
covenant with Moses is instituted, as is clear from the fact that Jews
have continued over the centuries to practice male circumcision. As
noted earlier, the same is true of the covenant with Noah, even though
it is not explicitly called eternal.

For P the most important covenant was the one initiated on
Mount Sinai between God and Israel through Moses. The covenants
with Noah and Abraham are, in one sense, merely preludes to this
third covenant. Its significance is indicated by the length of the section
P devotes to it. While the covenants with Noah and Abraham are
each related in a single chapter or less, the account of Israel's time at
Sinai encompasses half the book of Exodus (chapters 20—40), the
entire book of Leviticus, and most of Numbers 1—10, a total of 58
chapters! All of this material is set in the context of God's making a
covenant with Israel, and almost all of it is P. This material resembles
Deuteronomy in that most of it is law. The entire legal collection is
the law of the covenant, furnishing, as in Deuteronomy, the
stipulations of the covenant. Also, as in Deuteronomy, there is a section
of blessings and curses near the end of the law code (Lev. 26). The
blessing of the covenant is found there. Leviticus 26:9, quoted in the
chart above, contains language similar to the blessings of the Noachic
and Abrahamic covenants and may be considered the heart of that
blessing. But perhaps all of Leviticus 26:1–13 could be regarded as
the blessing of this covenant. The sign of the covenant, as explained
in Exodus 31:12–17, is the Sabbath. That passage also refers to this
covenant, like the covenant with Noah, as an eternal (NRSV
"perpetual") one.

Another indication of the importance of the Sinai covenant for P
is that he uses two different words for it. In addition to the usual
term, *bᵉrît*, P introduces another word, *ʿēdût*. The latter has a very
specific meaning for P. He uses it only for the Sinai covenant and
even more narrowly for the Ten Commandments. The word is sometimes translated "testimony" and apparently refers to the Decalog as
the tangible witness (the root meaning of the word) or attestation of
the covenant relationship between God and Israel. Thus, the stone

tablets on which the Ten Commandments are inscribed are frequently called the "tablets of the covenant (*'ēdût*)" by P (Exod. 31:18; 32:15; 34:29). Since the ark holds the tablets, it is known in P, as in Deuteronomy, as the "ark of the covenant"; only in P it is the word *'ēdût* that is used in the expression rather than *b'rît* (Exod. 25:22; 26:33–34; 30:6, 26; 39:35; 40:3, 5, 21; Num. 4:5; 7:89). By the same token, the tabernacle in which the ark with its tablets resides may be called the "tabernacle of the covenant" (*mishkan 'ēdût*, Exod. 38:21; Num. 1:50, 53). This last expression is particularly significant because it reflects the purpose of the covenant in P. If Israel will follow the covenant stipulations laid out in the law, then Yahweh will reside[12] in their midst. "I will place my dwelling in your midst...I will walk among you, and will be your God, and you shall be my people" (Lev. 26:11–12, NRSV).

Conclusions: Covenant in P and Dtr Compared

Many of the observations we made about covenant in Deuteronomy and the Deuteronomistic History apply also to P. It is appropriate still to speak of covenant as divine commitment and human obligation. P's covenants with Noah and Abraham both contain strong promissory elements, but each also imposes an obligation on the human partner in the form of the law of the covenant—the command not to eat or shed blood, in the case of Noah, and circumcision in the covenant with Abraham. Indeed, in P's usage "covenant" seems to have less of a sense of mutuality than in Deuteronomistic usage. P uses the term *b'rît* to refer to the promises not to destroy the world by flood (Gen. 9:9, 11) and to multiply Abraham's descendants and give them the land (Gen. 17:2, 4, 7–8). But then *b'rît* is also used specifically for the obligation of circumcision. One might say, therefore, that in P *b'rît* is divine commitment *or* (rather than *and*) human obligation. As for P's other word, *'ēdût,* since it is used exclusively of the Ten Commandments, it seems to refer solely to the human commitment side of the equation.

The ancient Near Eastern treaty still seems to be in the background of the Mosaic covenant in P, since it includes a set of curses

---

[12]The verb means to reside temporarily or in a temporary or mobile structure. It expresses at once the divine immanence and transcendence. Yahweh's permanent dwelling is in heaven; he only "tents" or "tabernacles" with his people.

(Lev. 26) as in Deuteronomy. But the treaty form does not lie behind the covenants with Noah and Abraham at all, nor is it really the model for P's Mosaic covenant. Thus, there are instructions about placing the tablets of the covenant ('*ēdût*) into the ark (Exod. 25:21), as was done with treaty documents. But the tablets bear only the Decalog and not, for example, the list of curses, so that they are not the same as a treaty document.

As in the Deuteronomistic History, P recounts a series of covenants. The covenants we surveyed in the Deuteronomistic History, however, are actually renewals of the one covenant with Israel at Horeb (Sinai in P). The book of Deuteronomy focuses on the renewal of this covenant at the end of Moses' life on the plains of Moab. Then, 2 Kings 23 relates the renewal of the same covenant under Josiah. P was written after the Deuteronomistic History as a kind of introduction to it. P accepted, and in a sense incorporated, Dtr's covenant history. But P also wished to add a history of the covenant before Sinai. P agreed with the Deuteronomistic History that the covenant at Horeb/Sinai was God's ultimate relationship with Israel. It could be renewed but not replaced. In P's scheme this covenant was preceded by covenants with Noah and Abraham. Unlike the covenants in the Deuteronomistic History, however, these were separate covenants rather than renewals of one original covenant. Nevertheless, P and Dtr agree—and P says explicitly—that God's covenants are eternal. The covenant with Noah remains in effect when the one with Abraham is instituted, and both of them continue when the Mosaic covenant comes along. The new covenants do not do away with the older one(s). The newer covenants do deal with more circumscribed groups of people. Noah's covenant was with all people, Abraham's only with him and his descendants, and the covenant under Moses only with Israelites or Jews (cf. Gen. 21:4). As in Deuteronomy, there are rewards and punishments for keeping or breaking the covenant. For P, the main reward is Yahweh's presence with Israel; the main punishment is his abandonment of them. But also for P, even more than for the Deuteronomistic writer(s), the covenant has not been abrogated and remains a source of hope for Israel in the exile.

4

OLD CURSES AND NEW COVENANT
Covenant in the Hebrew Prophets

O f all the writers behind the Bible, the prophets may be the least understood. Modern readers generally think that their function was to foretell the future. Christians in particular usually consider them forecasters of the coming of Jesus and the details of his life. This misimpression is partly the result of the New Testament's frequent citation of the Hebrew Bible materials in support of its interpretation of Jesus as the Messiah. But the whole idea of a coming Messiah developed for the most part "between the Testaments," that is, after the Hebrew Bible had been written. Furthermore, this Messiah was a political figure ("messiah" means "anointed" in Hebrew and was a title that could be used for any king) who was commonly expected to throw off the shackles of the Romans and reestablish the empire of David. Thus, in the New Testament, Jesus has to overcome this expectation among his followers and convince them that his kingdom is spiritual rather than political.

The primary role of prophets in the Hebrew Bible is best expressed in the adage that prophets are concerned more with *forthtelling* than with *foretelling*. Put another way, prophets were preachers who addressed the social, political, and religious circumstances of their day with a word from Yahweh. Their message is almost entirely negative. Prophetic oracles typically have two parts, one part that *denounces* the audience (usually the people of Israel or Judah with their leaders) and another that *announces* punishment. For example, the prophet Elijah tells King Ahab, "Because you have sold yourself to do what is evil in the sight of the LORD, I will bring disaster on you" (1 Kgs. 21:20–21, NRSV). The oracle goes on to describe the disaster in detail. Most oracles, especially in the prophetic books, are longer and more complex, but they still serve the same function of denouncing evildoing and announcing punishment.

The announcement of punishment is the part of the oracle that deals with the future. It is rarely specific about exactly when punishment is coming. Even the precise form that the punishment will take is not always clear. This is because different forms of disaster—plague, famine, military destruction, and so on—are envisioned. Rarely is the threat limited to one kind of disaster. What the prophets proclaim, therefore, amounts not to a prediction but to a threat. Indeed, they can be quite creative in the types of curses they invoke, as we will see in the next section. The announcement of punishment is also to be understood as conditioned upon the people's response to the oracle. It is, in effect, a threat of what God will do if the audience does not repent and change its ways. Thus, in Jeremiah 26 the prophet is arrested for treason and heresy after proclaiming that the temple in Jerusalem would be destroyed. His life is spared when some recall that Micah had preached much the same message a century earlier (Jer. 26:20; Mic. 3:12). Micah's words did not come true, but he was not considered a false prophet in Jeremiah's day. Rather, his threats were not fulfilled because they effected repentance among his hearers. Not only do the people of Jeremiah's day understand Micah's prophecy (and prophecy in general) as conditional, but they also perceive Micah (and prophets in general) to be speaking about his own time period, not hundreds of years in the future.

In another passage (28:8–9), Jeremiah reminds his hearers (and readers) of the very point we have been making here—that the message of prophets in the Hebrew Bible is mostly negative. Jeremiah even suggests that this is the test of a true prophet. It is the false prophets who prophesy peace when there is none (Jer. 6:14). Jeremiah says that when a prophet forecasts peace and it really comes, that prophet will be a true prophet indeed (28:9). We will see below that Jeremiah himself did look forward to a time of blessing in the form of a "new covenant" between God and his people, but that this would come only after destruction. Following this order, we will look next at the kinds of disasters the prophets threatened, drawing in part on treaty curses, and then at the time of renewal that they hoped for beyond devastation.

Treaty Curses and the Old Testament Prophets

The title of this section is borrowed from the dissertation of a well-known Old Testament scholar named Delbert Hillers, who studied and then taught for decades at Johns Hopkins University.[1] As the title of his book indicates, Hillers compared the curses found in various treaties from the ancient Near East with the threats leveled by the prophets of the Hebrew Bible. He sought to show that the prophets made use of the covenant as a common form of document and that, even though the eighth-century prophets rarely spoke of covenant, they were familiar with the idea as an expression of the relationship between God and Israel.

Hillers isolated twenty types of curses in the prophetic writings that he thought had probably originated as covenantal curses: (1) the land (or city) as the dwelling place of animals (due to the scarcity of people); (2) devouring animals; (3) removal of joyful sounds; (4) removal of the sound of millstones; (5) to become a prostitute; (6) to be stripped like a prostitute; (7) breaking of weapons; (8) breaking the scepter; (9) dry breasts; (10) to eat the flesh of sons and daughters; (11) ravishing of wives; (12) contaminated water; (13) incurable wound; (14) warriors become women; (15) no burial; (16) like a bird in a trap; (17) flood; (18) lack of men; (19) Sodom and Gomorrah; (20) passers-by will shudder.

---

[1] Hillers, *Treaty-Curses and the Old Testament Prophets*. BibOr 16. (Rome: Pontifical Biblical Institute, 1964).

Hillers' study fits with the sketch that we have drawn in previous chapters of the origin of covenant in Israel. All the treaties with which Hillers compares the prophetic material, except one, date from the eighth century or later. (The one exception is from the last quarter of the ninth century.) This is because, as we noted in chapter 2, the list of curses was characteristic of the Assyrian treaties, but not earlier ones. It means the covenant between God and Israel in the form that the Bible presents it could not have arisen much earlier than the eighth-century prophets. Hillers estimates that as many as one-half of the parallels he finds with the ancient Near Eastern treaties come from the sections of the prophetic books that contain oracles against foreign nations, and that these are among the closest parallels. Thus, the type of covenant with which the prophets were most familiar was the treaty between nations. This is not surprising, since such treaties were widespread in the ancient Near East, and the prophets seem to have been quite familiar with international relations.

As for the other 50 percent (or more) of the parallels, they do not necessarily indicate that the prophets have in mind a covenant between God and Israel. Certainly prophets such as Jeremiah and Ezekiel, who wrote at the same time or after the book of Deuteronomy, did assume the existence of this covenant. But for the earlier eighth-century prophets, the situation is more complicated. The prophets basically condemn Israel and Judah for social and religious offenses. They then threaten the offenders with destruction. Of course, the disasters from which the prophets drew their threats were those that were commonly feared by people of the ancient Near East and that also provided the content of covenantal curses. These included such horrors as drought, famine, disease, conquest, and captivity. Curses that were unrealistic would have been useless, so the events that the curses threatened were part of everyday life and were certainly not limited to covenants. The threat of nonburial, for instance, is found throughout the books of 1 and 2 Kings (1 Kgs. 14:11; 16:4; 21:23–24; 2 Kgs. 9:10, 30–37) and in the story of David and Goliath (1 Sam. 17:43–46), where there is no covenant. Similarly, the blessing of breasts and womb in Genesis 49:25, which is not in the context of a covenant, indicates that the threat of dry breasts in Hosea 9:14 may simply draw on a common repertoire (or life experience) without presupposing a covenant between God and Israel. In addition, the prophets' threats are sometimes metaphorical and therefore not the same as the covenantal curses. Thus, the main passages that Hillers cites as parallels to the curse of being stripped like a prostitute (Jer. 13:22–27; Ezek. 16; 23; Hos. 2) use the metaphor of Israel as an unfaithful wife and do not refer to actual women. Likewise, the flood in Isaiah 8:7 is a metaphor for the invasion of the Assyrian army, not an actual flood.

In sum, the threats of destruction that the biblical prophets utter do not disprove our contention that the covenant between God and Israel in the Bible effectively began with Deuteronomy. Even if an eighth-century prophet like Hosea did refer to such a covenant, the idea was not widespread nor the contents of the covenant widely agreed upon. This changed with the promulgation of Deuteronomy, so that the later prophets, especially Jeremiah and Ezekiel, could and did assume a general understanding of the nature of the covenant between Yahweh and Israel.

The Covenant as Marriage

The metaphor of marriage for the relationship of God and Israel is especially common and forceful in its use by the prophets. The metaphor is appropriate as an arrangement between two parties that binds them to one another. The prophet Malachi explicitly calls marriage a covenant between husband and wife (3:14–16). As we saw in the first chapter of this book, the earliest covenants, in a sense, were marriages. That is, covenants between families, clans, and tribes were sealed and represented by marriages. As an analogy for the relationship of Yahweh and his people, therefore, marriage was more natural than covenant and was available long before the covenant idea proper was conceived. Thus, Hosea's own marriage is used to represent the relationship of Yahweh to Israel without Hosea's referring explicitly to a covenant between them (Hos. 1—3). Again, as we saw in chapter 1, the idea of a covenant of God with Israel was not common in Hosea's day and may not even have been conceived at that time. The situation was different for Ezekiel, who twice used the marriage metaphor for God and Israel/Judah (Ezek. 16; 23), the first time referring to it explicitly and repeatedly as a covenant (16:8, 59, 60, 61, 62).

Several features of marriage are ideal analogues for the relationship of Yahweh and his people. It allows for the expression of Yahweh's love for Israel and brings home the exclusive nature of the relationship. Just as marriage partners typically vow to be faithful to each other and not take other lovers, so Israel is not to worship other gods. However, as used by the prophets, the marriage analogy has some unfortunate implications for modern readers. This is because the prophets used the analogy of marriage to condemn Israel's unfaithfulness, and they did so within the patriarchal society of ancient Israel. The sometimes graphic portrait of Israel as the whorish wife (especially Ezek. 16 and 23) may serve to reinforce misogyny among its audience members. Nevertheless, the analogy brings alive a sense of emotional trauma and hurt on God's part at the disloyalty of Israel that the image of covenant alone is unable to communicate.

The New Covenant

The concept of the new covenant in the Hebrew Bible must be seen in the light of the above information about prophets in order to be properly understood. As mentioned, the prophets sometimes envisioned a time of renewal in the future, but this time would only come after the punishment, in the form of destruction and devastation, was imposed. The time of renewal was typically described by the prophet in glowing, idealistic terms—what has appropriately been referred to as "utopian."[2] The prophet was expressing hope or a wish, rather than foretelling the future. Such oracles were often intended to inspire hope among those currently undergoing the sufferings the prophet had earlier threatened.

Jeremiah 31

Jeremiah's "new covenant" oracle is of this nature (Jer. 31: 31–34).

> "The days are coming," oracle of Yahweh, "when I will cut a covenant with the house of Israel and with the house of Judah—a new covenant—not like the covenant that I cut with their ancestors when I took them by the hand to bring them out of the land of Egypt, when they broke my covenant even though I was master over them," oracle of Yahweh. "But this is the covenant that I will cut with the house of Israel after those days," oracle of Yahweh, "I will place my

---

[2]Robert P. Carroll, *Jeremiah: A Commentary* (OTL; Philadelphia: Westminster Press, 1986), 612.

law inside of them; upon their heart I will write it. I will be their God and they will be my people. They will not need to teach each other or say to one another, 'Know Yahweh,' because all of them, from the least to the greatest, will know me," oracle of Yahweh. "For I will forgive their guilt, and their sin I will no longer remember."

It may come as a surprise to learn that this is the only place in the entire Hebrew Bible where the expression "new covenant" occurs. The new covenant is simply not a major theme in the Hebrew Bible. Furthermore, Jeremiah's new covenant does not refer to the New Testament or to Christianity, though it has often been interpreted this way. Jeremiah is not predicting the future. He does not give a specific time or date for the fulfillment of this oracle. He simply couches it in terms of the unknown future—"the days [that] are coming." It is a utopian vision.

The covenant that Jeremiah envisions is not a brand new covenant.[3] It is better understood, like those in the Deuteronomistic History, as a renewed covenant. This covenant, after all, involves the same partners; it is Yahweh's covenant with Israel and Judah—the descendants of the exodus generation, who were the recipients of the original covenant. Moreover, this covenant has the same law as the original one. What is new about the covenant Jeremiah envisions is its reception on the part of the Israelites. This covenant is not simply external but is inscribed on their hearts, and it will not, therefore, be broken as was the first one.

The marriage analogy can help to make the nature of this "new covenant" understandable. Indeed, Jeremiah may actually employ the analogy in this passage. The verb translated "I was master" above (v. 32) could be translated "I was husband" (NRSV). A marriage in which one of the partners is unfaithful does not have to end even though the marriage "covenant" has been violated. The marriage can continue, the vows and the relationship can be renewed. So with the new covenant in Jeremiah, it is not the covenant per se that is fundamentally different, but the human covenant partner who has changed.

---

[3]Cf. William McKane, *A Critical and Exegetical Commentary on Jeremiah*, 2, *Jeremiah XXVI–LII* (ICC; Edinburgh: T. & T. Clark, 1996), 818. McKane cites the great Jewish scholar Rabbi Kimchi as stating that "not like the covenant" in Jeremiah 31:32 means "the Sinai covenant fundamentally changed" rather than "not the [Sinai] covenant."

Hosea 2

Hosea does not refer to the new covenant as such, but he describes the renewal of God's relationship with Israel in terms of marriage. Hosea's own marriage is used to symbolize that of Yahweh and his people: "Yahweh said to Hosea, 'Go, take for yourself a wife and children of harlotry, for the land commits harlotry by not following Yahweh'" (1:2). His children's names symbolize the deterioration of the relationship: Jezreel—the site of the bloody coup that seated the present dynasty on Israel's throne; *Lo-Ruhamah*—"not loved"; *Lo-Ammi*—"not my people." With the naming of the third child comes an announcement of divorce: "For you are not my people and I AM not yours" (1:8). This statement is a renunciation of Yahweh's self-revelation, "I AM who I AM" in Exodus 3:14. A description of the coming punishment follows in Hosea 2:1–13 [Heb. vv. 3–16].

But then in the rest of chapter 2 Yahweh promises a renewal of the marriage. It is not a completely new marriage or relationship, because Israel will respond as "she" did the first time fresh out of Egypt (2:15 [Heb. v. 17]). The contrast is with Israel's current behavior. In contrast to the present, the Israel of the renewed marriage will not join with Baal (2:16–17 [Heb. vv. 18–19]) nor be plagued by internal injustice (2:19 [Heb v. 21]). It will be a time of perfect harmony such that even nature will be affected (2:18 [Heb. v. 20])—an obviously utopian vision.

Ezekiel

Like Hosea, Ezekiel also describes hope for the future in the context of a marriage. Working during the exile when Israel and Judah have received the punishment threatened by earlier prophets, Ezekiel uses the image of marriage in chapter 16 to review the history of Yahweh's relationship with his people, as we saw above. At the end of that review Ezekiel looks forward to a time of renewal. Unlike Hosea, Ezekiel expresses this renewal specifically as a covenant. Twice (16:60, 62) Yahweh promises to establish a covenant—an eternal covenant (v. 60)—with them. But this is certainly not a brand new arrangement. Yahweh contrasts his behavior as a covenant partner with that of Israel. Whereas they "despised the oath, breaking the covenant" (v. 59), Yahweh will remember his covenant (v. 60). Indeed, in this context "covenant" seems to mean "promise." Yahweh says that he will keep his part of the bargain, even though Israel has broken hers.

Israel will know by his faithfulness that he is Yahweh (v. 62). In short, there is not really a new covenant here at all, but rather an affirmation that God will carry out his promises from the original covenant despite Israel's failure to carry out its obligations.

There are three other references to a future covenant in the book of Ezekiel (34:25; 37:26 [twice]). All three are utopian in that they envision an ideal time of harmony in the future—a "covenant of peace." The context of 34:25 is similar to that of Hosea 2:18 [Heb. v. 20] in its description of the utter tranquility and fertility of nature. Both 34:25 and 37:26 envision the reunification of Israel and Judah as a single nation under King David. Their description of the covenant as an eternal one seems to be a democratization of the Davidic covenant, which will be discussed in detail in our next chapter.

2 Isaiah

Second (or Deutero-) Isaiah is the name given by scholars to chapters 40—55 of the book of Isaiah. These chapters presume a much different time period than the eighth century, the time of the original prophet Isaiah. Chapters 40—55 refer to the Babylonian exile as having been completed (40:2) and envision the imminent return of the captives from Babylon to Jerusalem (e.g., 40:3–5; 42:1–12). They also mention Cyrus, king of Persia, who assumed power in 539 B.C.E., as being on the throne (45:1). The entire "book" of 2 Isaiah, then, was written near the end of the exile (539–538 B.C.E.). It is uncharacteristically optimistic as it looks forward to the return of the people of Judah to their homeland, an event that it describes in glowing, utopian terms.

There are four mentions of covenant in 2 Isaiah: 42:6; 49:8; 54:10; 55:3.[4] The first two of these contain the identical expression "covenant of the people," which is unusual and does not occur elsewhere. Both the meaning of this expression and the interpretation of these

---

[4]There are also two mentions of covenant in the even later Third (Trito-) Isaiah, chapters 56—66: 59:21; 61:8. These do not add significantly to the understanding of covenant derived from the other prophetic texts, and so I have chosen not to discuss them at length both for the sake of brevity and convenience and because 3 Isaiah is so difficult to date and contextualize. The covenant in 59:21 is a promise of Yahweh's abiding presence. It is reminiscent of Jeremiah's new covenant in that Yahweh's spirit and words remain with the people and their heirs as Jeremiah's covenant is "cut" upon their hearts. The eternal covenant in 61:8 is part of a utopian vision of Israel's future that involves peace and prosperity for those who have suffered (cf. vv. 1–7).

verses are uncertain. In both cases, it is apparently Yahweh's "servant"[5] who is addressed. Oddly, the servant is called a covenant. The sense seems to be that the servant is the pledge that Yahweh will fulfill his promise to restore the people from exile.[6] What is important for our present concern is that this passage does not give a prediction of a new covenant in the distant future, but is based on the past relationship of God and Israel and concerns the immediate historical circumstance of the end of the exile and the impending return to the homeland.

The message of the other two covenant passages in 2 Isaiah is similar. In 54:9–10 the point is the permanence of Yahweh's promises. Just as God has kept his promise not to destroy the world again by flood, so will he keep his "covenant of peace." Although this expression is not defined here, it apparently refers to something similar to what Ezekiel meant by it (see above). Again covenant is promissory. The covenant of peace is God's promise to bring peace—rest, harmony, and prosperity—to his people as he brings them back from exile. Similarly, in 55:3 the permanence of the covenant is stressed, but the model has changed. It is no longer the covenant with Noah that is cited but the covenant with David. Just as Yahweh kept his eternal covenant with David and exalted him and his kingdom, so the exiles can rest assured that he will not only restore them to their land but will exalt them for the sake of his name. As in Ezekiel, the Davidic covenant is democratized and applied to the people as a whole. In the next chapter we will explore the nature of the covenant with David in detail.

Conclusions

The prophets were spokespersons or messengers for God to their contemporaries in Israel and Judah. They threatened impending disaster as a consequence for social injustice and religious apostasy. They

---

[5]Scholars have identified four passages in 2 Isaiah that they generally treat together as the "servant songs" because of their focus on Yahweh's servant. These are: 42:1–4; 49:1–6; 50:4–11; 52:13—53:12. The identity of the servant in these texts is disputed, with some seeing him as the nation of Israel, others as an individual; still others contend that the identity of the servant varies from song to song.

[6]Another possible interpretation, especially in 42:6, where "covenant of the people" is parallel to "light of the nations," is that the nation of Israel is somehow an agent of God's blessing to all people. This fits well with the universalism found elsewhere in 2 Isaiah but not as well with the more immediate context, which concerns the return from exile.

drew their threats from a repertoire of curses based on experiences of devastation in the ancient Near East. Such curses were used in international treaties from the eighth century and later. The prophets were familiar with such treaties and may have borrowed curses from them. However, the earlier prophets, Hosea in particular, did not necessarily presuppose a covenant between Yahweh and Israel already in the eighth century or borrow curses from that covenant. Later prophets, such as Jeremiah and Ezekiel, clearly do presuppose this covenant.

Beyond devastation, the prophets envision a time of renewal. Jeremiah alone describes this as a "new covenant"; the other prophets use different images, such as marriage. In all cases, including Jeremiah, it is not a brand new relationship that is envisioned. The partners are the same—God and Israel—as are the terms of the relationship. What is different is the faithful and obedient response of Israel. This period of renewal is always viewed in idealistic, "utopian" terms as a time of universal harmony and ultimate prosperity in Israel. For 2 Isaiah it is the imminent return from captivity and Israel's (Judah's) subsequent future that is cast in such a hopeful light. The prophets did not, therefore, foretell the future in any specific, realistic sense. However, it is easy to see how this utopian vision could be interpreted in a spiritual sense by Christianity.

5

"For the Sake of My Servant"
The Covenant with David

The Davidic covenant is one of the most complicated and controversial topics in the Hebrew Bible. This chapter will discuss the major aspects of the covenant with David by examining the key passages relating to it. These are:

1. a series of passages in the Deuteronomistic History—the fundamental text in 2 Samuel 7 and subsequent texts that relate to it (especially 2 Sam. 23:5; 1 Kgs. 8:15–26; 9:1–9; 15:4–5; 2 Kgs. 8:19);
2. the parallels to the Deuteronomistic passages in Chronicles: 1 Chronicles 17 (//2 Sam. 7); 2 Chronicles 6:4–17 (//1 Kgs. 8:15–26); and 2 Chronicles 7:12–22 (//1 Kgs. 9:1–9); plus other texts in Chronicles that refer to the covenant with David— 1 Chronicles 22:12–13; 28:7–10; and 2 Chronicles 21:7;
3. one passage in Jeremiah (33:14–26);
4. Psalms 89 and 132.

A Promissory Covenant
2 Samuel 7 and the Deuteronomistic History

The fundamental text for any consideration of the Davidic covenant is 2 Samuel 7, which is perhaps the most discussed passage in the Bible. David comes up with the idea of building a house (temple), and Nathan tells him to do all that he has in mind. But Yahweh has a different response. He does not accept David's idea, but he doesn't exactly reject it either. He asks David, "Is it *you* who will build a house for me to dwell in?" (7:5); the pronoun "you" is emphatic. After explaining that he has never demanded a house (vv. 6–7), Yahweh recounts his elevation of David from shepherd to king (vv. 8–11a) and then declares that he will build a house for David (v. 11b). "House" here refers to the continuation of David's line. It is David's son and successor who will build the temple (v. 13), and Yahweh promises to establish their dynasty (again, "house") forever (vv. 13, 16). It is this promise of an eternal royal line that essentially constitutes the covenant with David.

Second Samuel 7 is Dtr's composition.[1] As one author has put it, the chapter "fairly swarms" with recognized Deuteronomistic expressions.[2] Some of the clearest examples are the following:

> vv. 1, 11: Yahweh's giving rest from surrounding enemies[3]
> vv. 3, 9: "Yahweh is with you"
> v. 5: "my servant David"
> v. 6: Yahweh's bringing the Israelites up from Egypt
> vv. 9, 23: to make a [great] name
> v. 10: to appoint a place for Israel and plant them where
>   they will not be afflicted any more by evildoers [several
>   expressions combined here]

---

[1] This is a controversial claim. There have been numerous attempts to recover earlier layers in 2 Samuel 7, but none have achieved consensus, and in my view the effort is fatally flawed from the beginning because of the recognized fact that Dtr permeates the chapter. See my article "Why Didn't God Let David Build the Temple? The History of a Biblical Tradition," in M. Patrick Graham, Rick R. Marrs, and Steven L. McKenzie, eds., *Worship in the Old Testament: Essays in Honour of John T. Willis* (JSOTSup 284; Sheffield: Sheffield Academic Press, 1998), 204–24.

[2] Cross, *Canaanite Myth and Hebrew Epic,* 252. The following sample of such expressions is taken from Cross's list on pp. 252–54. However, Cross also argues for an earlier level of writing preserved in the chapter.

[3] But 7:1b is probably a late addition because it causes contradictions with other parts of the Deuteronomistic History. See my discussion in the article cited in n. 1.

v. 13: "a house [temple] for my name"

v. 16: a sure house

v. 23: Yahweh's redeeming Israel through great and awe-
some things

The Deuteronomistic nature and origin of the Davidic promise
is further indicated by the fact that it becomes an important theme in
the rest of the Deuteronomistic History.[4] Solomon alludes to it in his
prayer at the dedication of the temple in 1 Kings 8 (vv. 24–26), and
Yahweh reiterates the promise to Solomon when he appears to the
new king at Gibeon (1 Kgs. 9:4–5). David becomes the standard by
which subsequent kings of Judah are judged. Hence, Solomon did
not walk "in my ways doing what is right in my eyes…as did David
his father" (1 Kgs. 11:33). Abijam's "heart was not true to Yahweh his
God as was the heart of David his father" (1 Kgs. 15:3). Asa "did
what was right in Yahweh's eyes as did David his father" (1 Kgs. 15:11).
Amaziah "did what was right in Yahweh's eyes, though not like David
his father" (2 Kgs. 14:3), and Ahaz "did not do what was right in the
eyes of Yahweh his God as did David his father" (2 Kgs. 16:2). But
Hezekiah "did what was right in the eyes of Yahweh according to all
that David his father had done" (2 Kgs. 18:3). Josiah also "walked in
all the way of David his father without turning to the right or the
left" (2 Kgs. 22:2).

It is David's faithfulness and/or Yahweh's promise that prolongs
Judah's existence. Because of Solomon's sin, Yahweh took Israel away
from the Davidic line of rulers. He left them Judah and did not effect
the division until after Solomon, all "for the sake of David" (1 Kgs.
11:11–12, 32–35), "so that my servant David will always have a domain[5] before me in Jerusalem, the city that I have chosen for myself
to place my name there" (11:36). These concessions are apparently
motivated by God's promise to David in 2 Samuel 7. They also show
how Jerusalem's fate is linked with that of the Davidic dynasty. Thus,
in a later episode during the reign of King Hezekiah, when Jerusalem

---

[4]As highlighted initially by Von Rad ("The Deuteronomistic Theology of History in the
Books of Kings," 74–91 in his *Studies in Deuteronomy*) and then by Cross ("The Themes of the
Book of Kings and Structure of the Deuteronomistic History," *Canaanite Myth and Hebrew
Epic*, 274–89).

[5]The usual translation of this word as "lamp" (NRSV) does not make much sense. The
translation here reflects the alternative meaning "fiefdom" suggested by Paul D. Hanson, "The
Song of Heshbon and David's *Nir*," *HTR* 61 (1968): 297–320.

is threatened by the Assyrian army, Yahweh twice states his intention to save the city "for my sake and for the sake of David my servant" (2 Kgs. 19:34; 20:6). Twice the writer (Dtr) explains that Jerusalem was not destroyed despite wicked kings "for David's sake": In 1 Kings 15:4 God gave Abijam a domain in Jerusalem "establishing his son after him and causing Jerusalem to stand," even though Abijam "walked in all the sins of his father" (v. 3). More explicit is 2 Kings 8:19, which says that even though Jehoram of Judah was as wicked as the infamous King Ahab of Israel, Yahweh would not destroy Judah for David's sake "because he had promised to give him a domain for his sons forever." The promise to David, therefore, is the reason that Judah and Jerusalem lasted as long as they did, according to the Deuteronomistic History.

Dtr never refers to God's promise to David as a "covenant" (b'rît). That term does not occur in 2 Samuel 7. In fact, there is only one reference to a "covenant" with David in the entire Deuteronomistic History. That reference is in 2 Samuel 23:5, which is part of a section of 2 Samuel (chapters 21—24) that is widely regarded by scholars as a later addition to the Deuteronomistic History. In addition, the poem known as "the last words of David" (2 Sam. 23:1–7) was probably a late composition from the time of the Babylonian exile (586–539 B.C.E.) or later.[6] The NRSV also uses the word "covenant" in 1 Kings 8:24 in the context of Solomon's prayer: "the covenant that you kept for your servant my father David as you declared to him." However, this translation is misleading, since the Hebrew word b'rît does not occur here. The verse actually begins with the relative "which" and is a continuation of the previous verse. The "which" does not necessarily refer to "covenant" in verse 23 but seems to be a more general reference to Yahweh's faithfulness or "steadfast love" (Hebrew ḥesed). The NRSV translation of the parallel verse in 2 Chronicles 6:15, which is exactly the same in Hebrew as 1 Kings 8:24, more accurately renders the sense: "you who have kept for your servant, my father David, what you promised to him."

---

[6]The poem is difficult to date, but a few vocabulary items indicate a late date. First, the expression "eternal covenant" in verse 5 occurs elsewhere in the Hebrew Bible only in passages from the seventh century on, as pointed out by T. N. D. Mettinger (*King and Messiah: The Civil and Sacral Legitimation of the Israelite Kings* [ConBOT 8; Lund: C. W. K. Gleerup, 1976], 257n). Second, the word *millatô* ("his word") in verse 2 is also late. See P. Kyle McCarter (*II Samuel* [AB 9; Garden City, N.Y.: Doubleday, 1984], 485), who acknowledges this but regards verse 2 as a later addition to an otherwise early composition.

It makes perfect sense that Dtr does not refer to God's promise to David as a covenant. For him there is only one covenant—the one given through Moses on Mount Horeb. After the time of Dtr, hence late in Israelite history, the promise to David was conceived of as a "covenant." We have already seen that 2 Samuel 23:5 was likely written in the exile or later. The same is true of the other passages in the Bible that express the idea of a Davidic "covenant." We will survey those passages next.

Chronicles

As with 2 Samuel, the Chronicles version of the promise to David through Nathan in 1 Chronicles 17 does not contain the word "covenant" (*bᵉrît*). But there are two texts in Chronicles that do refer to this promise as a covenant. The first is in the speech of Abijah, king of Judah, to the Israelite army in the middle of a civil war between Israel and Judah (2 Chr. 13:4–12). The speech is unique to Chronicles. It is the Chronicler's composition and reveals his theology, especially his attitude about the division between Israel and Judah and his view of the Israelites still as Yahweh's people though in apostasy. In verse 5 (NRSV) of that speech Abijah says, "Do you not know that the LORD God of Israel gave the kingship over Israel forever to David and his sons by a covenant of salt?" The expression "covenant of salt" is somewhat obscure, but it seems to mean a permanent covenant and apparently arose from the properties of salt as a preservative and from its use in ceremonial meals ratifying covenants. Judging from its occurrences in Chronicles and elsewhere, it is a late expression (Lev. 2:13; Num. 18:19—both P; cf. Ezra 4:14).

The second reference to a covenant with David in Chronicles is 2 Chronicles 21:7. This verse parallels the explanation of Judah's preservation in 2 Kings 8:19.

2 Kings 8:19	2 Chronicles 21:7
Yet Yahweh would not destroy Judah, for the sake of his servant David, since he had promised to give a dominion to him and to his sons forever.	Yet Yahweh would not destroy the house of David because of the covenant that he had made with David, and since he had promised to give a dominion to him and to his sons forever.

The differences between the two verses are obvious. Chronicles mentions the house of David, rather than Judah, as the object of Yahweh's preservation, and it explains that this is because of the covenant God had made with David. As in 2 Chronicles 13:5, therefore, we have a reference to the promise to David as a covenant, and both references can be directly attributed to the Chronicler interpreting the Deuteronomistic History.

Jeremiah 33:14–26

Jeremiah 33:14–26 is a late addition to the book of Jeremiah. This is indicated by the fact that this passage is missing from the Greek version (known as the Septuagint and abbreviated LXX) of Jeremiah.[7] The content of this passage also indicates its lateness. The oracle that begins in verse 14 looks forward to an undetermined point in the future ("days are coming," v. 14) when God "will cause a righteous shoot to sprout for David" (v. 15). The allusion is to the re-establishment of the Davidic monarchy, which means that at the time the oracle was spoken there was no king on David's throne. Similarly, verse 24 articulates the charge that God has rejected "the two families whom Yahweh chose." This refers either to the nations of Israel and Judah or to the tribes of Judah (David's tribe) and Levi. The two verses, then, presuppose the exile, and in fact seem to point to a time after the exile when hope for the restoration of the Davidic monarchy—in tandem with the Levitical priesthood—was current. The post-exilic date for the passage is further confirmed by the mention in verse 26 of the patriarchs, Abraham, Isaac, and Jacob, by name, which reflects an acquaintance with the Pentateuch more or less in its present form.[8]

Psalm 89

Psalm 89 was also written during the exile, at least in its present form. I say "in its present form" because some scholars consider the

---

[7]The LXX translation was probably done in the third century B.C.E. in Egypt. The Hebrew text that served as a basis for that translation is not that late but was likely brought from Palestine at an earlier date. See the next footnote.

[8]William L. Holladay (*Jeremiah 2: A Commentary on the Book of the Prophet Jeremiah Chapters 26—52* [Hermeneia; Minneapolis: Fortress Press, 1989], 228–30) gives other arguments for a late date and places this passage at about 400 B.C.E.

part of the psalm in verses 5–18 [Heb. 6–19] to be older, perhaps by quite a bit.[9] However, the complaint in verses 38–45 [Heb. 39–46] that Yahweh has now rejected the Davidic dynasty strongly suggests an exilic setting, when the king of Judah had been removed and the nation turned into the province of a foreign power. In addition, these verses are full of language and images that are common in literature from the exile or later, such as the book of Lamentations.[10] Examples include the references to God's spurning and rejecting his people or David as in verse 38 and his renouncing the covenant in verse 39a, the defiling of the crown in verse 39b, and the motif of the passers-by in verse 41, who not only mock but this time also plunder.

Psalm 89 has many ideas and expressions in common with 2 Samuel 7. These include:

> the reference to David as "my servant" (Ps. 89:20; 2 Sam. 7:5),
> the statement that the evidoer(s) will not afflict or humble the Davidic king (Ps. 89:23; 2 Sam. 7:10),
> the statement that Yahweh's "steadfast love" (*ḥesed*) will be with David or his son (Ps. 89:24, 28, 33; 2 Sam. 7:15),
> the reference to Yahweh as the Davidic king's father (Ps. 89:26; 2 Sam. 7: 14),
> the promise to establish David's "seed" and "throne" forever (Ps. 89:29, 36; 2 Sam. 7:12–13),
> the promise to discipline David's heir(s) as one would a child without removing "steadfast love" (*ḥesed)* (Ps. 89:30–33; 2 Sam. 7:14–15).

The parallels of Psalm 89 to other late texts show that the direction of influence must be from 2 Samuel to Psalm 89 rather than the

---

[9]For example, Cross contends that these verses (what he calls 89B) are ancient and that 89A and 89C in verses 2–4, 19–37 (Heb. 3–5, 20–38) come from the time of the monarchy (*Canaanite Myth and Hebrew Epic*, 97n, 257–62). While he does not discuss the final portion of the psalm, he would apparently date it to the exile, to judge from his typology on pp. 264–65. Similarly, Veijola's analysis of the psalm's structure leads him to conclude that verses 1–2 and 5–18 were the initial level of the psalm to which verses 3–4 and 19–45 and then even later verses 46–51 were added. See Timo Veijola, *Verheissung in der Krise: Studien zur Literatur und Theologie der Exilszeit anhand des 89. Psalms* (AASF B 220; Helsinki: Suomalainen Tiedeakatemia, 1992), 22–46. The case for the psalm's unity is presented by Richard J. Clifford, "Psalm 89: A Lament over the Davidic Ruler's Continued Failure," *HTR* 73 (1980): 35–47. But Clifford does not settle on a date for the psalm.

[10]Veijola (*Verheissung in der Krise*, 47–118) gives a comprehensive discussion of the language of the psalm. The examples that follow are taken from pp. 95–112 of his study.

other way around. The covenant with David in Psalm 89, in other words, is an interpretation of the promise to David in 2 Samuel 7.

This brief survey indicates that the very idea of the promise to David's being a *covenant* was a late one. (We might also mention Isa. 55:3, which was treated in the previous chapter, since its mention of the covenant with David stems from the late exilic writer known as Second Isaiah.) This fits well with the conclusion we reached in chapter 1 that the promissory covenant of God with Abraham in Genesis 15 is a late text. Perhaps God's promises to Abraham and David were designated as covenants as a way of emphasizing the "divine commitment" to the people of Israel, thereby providing a source of hope for restoration during and after the exile. We will explore this possibility in more detail below. But whatever the reason, the promise to David is called a covenant in the Bible, even if only in late texts. Hence, it calls for our further attention and analysis of its nature and its special features.

An Eternal Covenant

The passages just surveyed all refer in different ways to the promise or covenant with David as eternal. Thus, 2 Samuel 7:13 and 15 refer to David's throne, dynasty ("house"), and kingdom's being established forever, and this is echoed in 1 Kings 9:5. A different expression occurs in 1 Kings 11:36 and 2 Kings 8:19; in both passages David's line is assured a domain in Jerusalem "all the days." Although Jeremiah 33:14–26 does not use either of these expressions for the Davidic covenant, the whole point of the passage is that God will never break his covenants with David (esp. vv. 19–22) or the Levites (whose covenant is expressly for "all the days," v. 18). Psalm 89 repeatedly quotes Yahweh as saying that David's line (lit. "seed") and throne will be established forever (in vv. 28, 29, 36, and 37), and Psalm 132 agrees, saying that David's sons will sit on his throne "forevermore." Finally, Isaiah 55:3 also agrees that the agreement with David is an eternal covenant.

As we saw earlier, covenants were typically intended to be in perpetuity, so this feature is not unique to the Davidic covenant. Still, it is curious that the Davidic covenant is repeatedly and explicitly designated "eternal" while others, such as the Sinai covenant, are not. We must ask, therefore, what the exact sense of "forever" in these passages is. These matters are not as easy to resolve as one might initially think. Indeed, to some extent the definition varies with different authors.

It is worthwhile to observe at the outset that ancient Israelites did not have the same sense of, or belief in, eternity that modern Christians do. There was no view of an afterlife in heaven or hell, so that any idea of "forever" was limited to this world. Its sense, therefore, is really "for a very long time." It can be similar to what we mean today when we say, "I've been waiting for you *forever*." A good example from the Bible is 1 Chronicles 28:4 where David says that Yahweh took him from his father's house to be king over Israel *forever*. Here "forever" evidently refers to David's lifetime, since he goes on to explain that Solomon's kingdom will also last "forever" if he is obedient. Exactly how long "forever" was supposed to be when applied to David's dynasty was a matter over which biblical writers differed.

We begin again with Dtr. As we have seen, he used the Davidic promise to explain the endurance of Judah and its dynasty despite their sinfulness. Dtr nowhere hints that Judah's eventual fall contradicts the promise of an eternal Davidic dynasty. Yahweh kept his promise, and that is why Judah lasted as long as it did. For Dtr, therefore, "forever" meant the duration of the nation of Judah. Whether Dtr found any hope in the Davidic promise for the continuation of the dynasty and the nation in the future is a matter about which scholars disagree. Gerhard von Rad argued that the final passage of the Deuteronomistic History (2 Kgs. 25:27–30), which relates how King Jehoiachin of Judah was released from Babylonian prison, was Dtr's way of holding out a hint of hope, showing where Yahweh could start to restore his people.[11] But Dtr gives no explicit reason for believing that the promise of an "eternal"—or, perhaps better, an enduring—Davidic dynasty mandated its continuation beyond the exile.

For 1 and 2 Chronicles, the eternal covenant with David can only be understood in the context of its larger portrait of David and Solomon. Chronicles borrows heavily from the books of 2 Samuel and 1 and 2 Kings. But the Chronicler omitted almost all the negative

---

[11]Von Rad, "The Deuteronomistic Theology of History in the Books of Kings," in *Studies in Deuteronomy*, 90–91. Friedman, in contrast, has argued that these last four verses of 2 Kings are a later addition because they skip over some twenty-five years without comment. (See Richard E. Friedman, *The Exile and Biblical Narrative* [HSM 22; Chico, Calif.: Scholars Press, 1981], 35–36, and "From Egypt to Egypt: Dtr 1 and Dtr 2," in Baruch Halpern and Jon Levenson, eds., *Traditions in Transformation* [Winona Lake, Ind.: Eisenbrauns, 1981], 189–91.)

material about David and Solomon (including the story of David's sin with Bathsheba [2 Sam. 11—12] and the trouble that follows [2 Sam. 13–20] as well as the account of Solomon's sin [1 Kgs. 11]), so that they appear as model kings of Israel's "Golden Age."[12] The Chronicler also added descriptions of David as the one who instituted the liturgy of the future temple, provided the building materials for it, and appointed the priestly families in charge of administering it (1 Chr. 15—16 and 22—29). In speeches composed by the chronicler (esp. chap. 22 and 29), David explains that Solomon is the one chosen by God to build the temple. Here, he refers to the divine promise to establish Solomon's throne and kingdom "forever" (22:10; 28:7).

These same themes account for the subtle differences between the version of the promise to David in 1 Chronicles 17 and the version in 2 Samuel 7:

2 Samuel	1 Chronicles 17
v. 12: When your days are filled and you lie with your fathers, I will raise up your seed after you who will come from your loins and I will establish his kingdom.	v. 11: When your days are filled to walk with your fathers, I will raise up your seed after you, who will be one of your sons, and I will establish his kingdom.
v. 13: He will build a temple for my name and I will establish the throne of his kingdom forever.	v. 12: He will build a temple for me, and I will establish his throne forever.
v. 14: I will be a father to him and he will be a son to me; when he commits iniquity I will discipline him with the rod of men and with human blows	v. 13: I will be a father to him and he will be a son to me
v. 15: but I will not remove my steadfast love from him as I removed [it] from Saul whom I removed from before you.	and I will not remove my steadfast love from him as I removed it from the one who preceded you.
v. 16: Your dynasty and your kingdom will be firm forever before me; your throne will be sure forever.	v. 14: I will establish him in my house and in my kingdom forever and his throne will be sure forever.

---

[12]First Chronicles 21 does recount the story of David's sin in taking the census that comes from 2 Samuel 24. The apparent reason is that the story explained how the site for the altar in the temple was chosen (1 Chr. 21:28—22:1). The Chronicler attached such importance to the temple and its institutions that he was willing to tarnish David's reputation slightly in order to include this story.

The Chronicler makes clear that it is one of David's own sons who will succeed him (v. 14). David is exemplary for his faithfulness to Yahweh; Solomon is the builder of the temple (v. 12). Since Chronicles does not mention Solomon's sin, there is no need to raise the possibility of his committing iniquity in the future (v. 13) as in the Samuel version.

Chronicles, then, seems to be more ambiguous about the "eternal" nature of the Davidic promise than the Deuteronomistic History. As we saw earlier, in 1 Chronicles 28:4 "forever" refers to David's own lifetime. Other texts—1 Chronicles 17:14; 22:10; and 28:7— all mention an "eternal" throne or kingdom for Solomon and may be interpreted to mean either that Solomon himself will reign "forever" or that his dynasty will be "eternal." But 2 Chronicles 21:7, which was quoted above, refers explicitly to the Davidic covenant as promising David and his "sons" a domain (nîr) forever. This verse shows that the Chronicler understood the promise through Nathan to apply to the dynasty. In fact, the verse states that it is the dynasty ("house of David") that is saved from destruction rather than the nation of Judah as in 2 Kings 8:19. Perhaps this was because the Chronicler was aware that the royal line continued even though Judah no longer existed as a nation in his day. To the extent that he held up David and Solomon as models for the restoration of the kingship, the "eternal" Davidic covenant provided a source of hope for him for the future.

Other texts surveyed that refer to Dtr's Davidic promise as a covenant certainly interpret its eternal nature more or less literally. In Jeremiah 33:14–26 the "eternal" covenant with David is a source of hope for the restoration of the nation under a Davidic king in the future. This is because the covenant with David is as permanent and eternal as night and day (33:25). Thus, despite the exile, the covenant remains in effect. The author of Psalm 89 also takes the language of an eternal covenant literally. Like the other passages that interpret Dtr's Davidic promise as a covenant, Psalm 89 sees the covenant as still in effect during the exile and afterward, when Judah had lost its status as an independent nation under the rule of a Davidic king. But whereas the other passages view the endurance of the covenant of David as a source of hope for the restoration of kingdom and dynastic monarch, Psalm 89 uniquely complains that God has broken the covenant and his promise. The covenant was forever; it's just that Yahweh has not kept it.

An Unconditional Covenant?

Related to the eternal nature of the Davidic covenant is the question of its unconditionality. Some of the texts about the covenant explicitly describe it as unconditional. Thus, through Nathan, God tells David that when his son and successor sins, "I will discipline him with the rod of men and with human blows, but I will not remove my steadfast love from him...your dynasty and your kingdom will be firm forever before me; your throne will be sure forever" (2 Sam. 7:14–16). Psalm 89 echoes these words in poetic form:

> I will establish his seed forever
> and his throne like the lifetime [lit. "days"] of the
>   heavens.
> If his sons abandon my law
> and do not walk in my judgments,
> if they violate my statutes
> and do not keep my ordinances,
> then I will punish their transgression with a rod,
> their sin with blows.
> But my steadfast love I will not remove[13] from him,
> I will not falsify my faithfulness. (vv. 29–33)

Jeremiah 33:19–22 also refers to the Davidic covenant as unconditional in the sense that it cannot be broken by human means; God will maintain his commitment to it even if humans fail to fulfill their obligation.

However, other texts just as explicitly make the covenant with David conditional upon the obedience of David's descendants. Thus, David quotes Yahweh's promise in his deathbed charge to Solomon, "If your heirs take heed to their way, to walk before me in faithfulness with all their heart and with all their soul, there shall not fail you a successor on the throne of Israel" (1 Kgs. 2:4, NRSV). And Solomon quotes the same promise in nearly identical terms: "There shall not fail you a successor before me sitting on the throne of Israel, if only your heirs look to their way to walk before me as you walked before me" (1 Kgs. 8:25). Then the promise as reiterated to Solomon in

---

[13]Reading a form of the verb "remove" with 2 Samuel 7:15 and for the sake of sense preceding the prepositional phrase "from him" rather than the verb "break" that is in the Hebrew (Masoretic) text.

1 Kings 9:4–5 is conditional: "If you will walk before me as David your father walked…then I will establish the throne of your kingdom over Israel forever." The version of the promise given in Psalm 132 is also conditional: "If your sons keep my covenant and my decrees that I shall teach them, their sons also, forevermore, shall sit on your throne" (v. 12, NRSV).

Some scholars have explained this variation between conditional and unconditional characterizations by theorizing that there were different conceptions of the Davidic covenant at different periods and in different parts of ancient Israel. In one such theory, the original covenant with David was conditional, and the unconditional version arose with the Davidic empire as propaganda for its permanent rule over Judah.[14] Another theory holds that the covenant with David was originally unconditional and was modeled on the form of land grants made by kings to faithful servants; the element of conditionality was introduced by Dtr after the fall of Israel (721 B.C.E.) and then Judah (586 B.C.E.).[15] Both these theories assume the antiquity of the passages about the Davidic covenant. But as we have seen, the idea of a dynastic promise to David began with the Deuteronomistic History and was then interpreted as a covenant and in other respects by later writers.[16] Thus, in order to understand the variation between conditional and unconditional versions of the Davidic covenant, we must must begin once again with 2 Samuel 7 and the Deuteronomistic History.

The original promise in 2 Samuel 7 raises the possibility that David's heir will sin. Yahweh says he will punish the heir as a father disciplines his son but promises not to remove his "steadfast love" (*ḥesed*) from him as he did from Saul. Rather, David's dynasty and kingdom will remain sure forever (7:14–16). This promise is unconditional in the sense that Yahweh commits to giving David a dynasty

---

[14]Cross, *Canaanite Myth and Hebrew Epic,* 219–73.

[15]Moshe Weinfeld, "The Covenant of Grant in the Old Testament and in the Ancient Near East," *JAOS* 90 (1970): 184–203; and Weinfeld, "ברית berîth," *TDOT* 2: 270–72. For a critique of this view see Gary N. Knoppers, "Ancient Near Eastern Royal Grants and the Davidic Covenant: A Parallel?" *JAOS* 116 (1996): 670–97.

[16]The one text that is important for this discussion and whose date we have not yet established is Psalm 132. While it has been dated early, that is, to the time of David (cf. Cross in n. 9), it contains several examples of Deuteronomistic language (listed by Mettinger, *King and Messiah*, 256). It also presupposes the oracle of Nathan in 2 Samuel 7, which we have seen to be Dtr's work. Like the other texts we have treated, therefore, Psalm 132 is a late composition and interprets 2 Samuel 7.

even if his son sins. But what is on view here is specifically the accession and reign of Solomon, as the subsequent Deuteronomistic History makes clear. Hence, in his prayer in 1 Kings 8:24, Solomon notes that Yahweh has now fulfilled his promise to David in Solomon's succession (v. 20). He goes on to ask Yahweh to keep his word always to have a descendant of David on the throne if the descendants remain faithful (8:25; cf. 2:4). Thus, the promise about the rest of David's dynasty is conditional. When God reiterates the promise to Solomon in the next chapter (1 Kgs. 9:4–5), it is conditional and concerns the throne of Israel. These strands come together in 1 Kings 11—12. Solomon's sin, forecast in 2 Samuel 7, leads Yahweh to discipline him. This he does by taking away the throne over Israel, that is, the northern kingdom. In accord with his promise in 2 Samuel 7, he does not treat Solomon as he had Saul. Saul's line was cut off, but Solomon's continues to have a domain in Jerusalem and Judah—"for the sake of David" (1 Kgs. 11:11–13, 31–37). Jeroboam is also offered an eternal dynasty that is conditioned on his obedience (11:38). After this point, the promise of a Davidic dynasty is alluded to only twice (1 Kgs. 15:4; 2 Kgs. 8:19). Neither text is specific about whether the promise is conditional or unconditional, though the final demise of Judah would suggest that it was conditional. Yahweh's faithfulness to his promise accounted for Judah's endurance as a nation ("forever") but was never meant by Dtr to be a license for wickedness on the part of Judah's kings.

This interpretation of Dtr's use of the Davidic promise is confirmed by the parallels in Chronicles. As noted earlier, the Chronicles version of Nathan's oracle (2 Sam. 7//1 Chr. 17) omits the possibility that David's successor might sin. The Chronicler, therefore, is even more unconditional in this portion of the promise than Dtr. But the reason for the Chronicler's omission, as we have seen, is his idealization of Solomon. As with Dtr, the unconditional part of the promise relates only to Solomon. Later references in Chronicles to the Davidic covenant treat it as conditional just as in the Deuteronomistic History (2 Chr. 6:16//1 Kgs. 8:25; 2 Chr. 7:17–18//1 Kgs. 9:4–5).

The later references to the Davidic covenant in passages we have surveyed above interpret it along the same lines as they do the "eternal" nature of the covenant. Psalm 89 sees the covenant as unconditional. The psalm does this by applying the provision about Solomon's potential trespass to all of David's descendants. Thus, whereas 2 Samuel

7:14 says, "When *he* commits iniquity I will discipline *him* with the rod of men," Psalm 89:30 reads, "If his sons [plural] abandon my law ...I will punish *their* transgression with a rod." It is on this basis that the psalm complains that Yahweh has violated his covenant by rejecting the Davidic king. Jeremiah 33:14–26 also interprets the covenant as unconditional, since nothing the king or people do can break it; this is the writer's source of hope for the future. Psalm 132, on the other hand, is close to Dtr in its description of the promise to David as explicitly and uniquely conditional. It shares with Jeremiah 33 the perspective that the promise offers hope for the future. Yahweh's statement that he will cause a horn to sprout up for David in his chosen city of Jerusalem (v. 17) looks forward to the reestablishment of the Davidic dynasty at some point after the exile.

Typology of the Davidic Covenant

Some scholars have tried to sketch the typological development of the idea of a covenant with David, showing how it changed from the time of David himself through the history of the monarchy and into the exile.[17] Our treatment in this chapter has indicated a very different developmental history. The covenant with David began not as a covenant, but as a promise or oath in the account of Nathan's oracle in 2 Samuel 7. We cannot say for certain that Dtr originated the idea of this promise; it is possible that the idea was already current during the monarchy as propaganda supporting the Davidic dynasty. But there is no literary evidence of such a tradition in the Bible that can be convincingly traced to the time of the monarchy. The descriptions of the promise in the Deuteronomistic History are all in Deuteronomistic language. Also, the fact that the eighth-century prophets do not mention such a tradition suggests that it arose later. Whatever its origins, Dtr used the Davidic promise to account for the endurance of the Davidic dynasty and of Judah, both of which continued long after the nation of Israel had fallen to Assyria (721 B.C.E.). For Dtr, the promise to David was "eternal," as one would expect for all divine promises, but also conditional, depending on the behavior of the members of the dynasty. The only unconditional part of the promise was that concerning Solomon's retention of the kingship

---

[17]See especially Cross, *Canaanite Myth and Hebrew Epic*, 264–65.

despite his sin, and Dtr used this to anticipate Solomon's apostasy, by which Dtr explained the division of the kingdom following his reign.

Subsequent biblical writers called the promise to David a covenant, and they interpreted it in different ways.[18] There was, therefore, not a single typological development but a variety of understandings of the covenant's significance. Chronicles and Psalm 132 are both close in outlook to the Deuteronomistic History. The Chronicler uses the term "covenant" for God's promise to David, while Psalm 132 does not. But both agree with Dtr in describing it as eternal and conditional. For both writers the covenant with David furnished hope for restoration in the future. Jeremiah 33:14–26 also found a source of hope in the Davidic covenant, precisely because, for this late author, the covenant was unconditional as well as eternal. The author of Psalm 89 also saw the covenant as eternal and unconditional and registered a complaint on just those grounds. Contrary to his promise, Yahweh had allowed the Davidic dynasty to fall; the unique claim of this writer was that God had broken his covenant. The Davidic covenant, therefore, spawned both hope and despair in ancient Israel.

It may be frustrating to some readers to find that there is disagreement among the biblical writers about the nature of the Davidic covenant. This variety of understandings in some ways epitomizes the Hebrew Bible and is the essence of its complexity and sophistication. On many such themes the Hebrew Bible offers different perspectives as authors struggle with theological issues. It is appropriate, therefore, that we end our discussion of covenant in the Hebrew Bible precisely at the point where two of its greatest themes converge. These two themes are covenant and theodicy. That latter word literally means "God's justice" and is the problem presented by the presence of evil and suffering in a world created by an all-good, all-powerful God.

The different interpretations of the Davidic covenant coincided with different perspectives on the crisis of the exile. The nation of Judah and the Davidic monarchy were brought to an end. The city of Jerusalem was destroyed. There was widespread destruction of homes and property and extensive loss of life. Some survivors became captives

---

[18]For more on the variety of interpretation of the Davidic covenant, especially its (un)conditionality, see Gary N. Knoppers, "David's Relation to Moses: The Contexts, Content and Conditions of the Davidic Promises," in John Day, ed., *King and Messiah in Israel and the Ancient Near East: Proceedings of the Oxford Old Testament Seminar* (JSOTSup 270; Sheffield: Sheffield Academic Press, 1998), 91–118.

in a foreign land (Babylon); others remained in an impoverished homeland. Why? Was it because of human sin, and did the leaders bear a greater responsibility for it than the common people? These were Dtr's claims, and he further asserted that Judah had lasted as long as it did because of Yahweh's loyalty to David. Dtr's response was the most influential, but it was not the only one. A different response was voiced by Psalm 89, which boldly asked why God, not humans, had broken his covenant. (The book of Job may offer yet another response—that God has his reasons, which humans cannot understand.)

Most of the texts we have studied in this chapter, however, focus on a different aspect of theodicy. Whatever the cause of the exile, they ask, What now? The authors of Chronicles, Jeremiah 33:14–26, Psalm 132, and other texts look to the nature of the God in whom they believe. They put their trust not in "God's justice" but in God's mercy and God's loyalty. These authors find hope for the future in the divine commitment to David. They thereby place their trust not in the nation, its government, or its institutions, but in God. These writers would likely agree with the sentiment expressed in 1 Chronicles 17:14 that the dynasty and the nation belong to Yahweh. They believe that God is supremely powerful; they put their trust in his goodness to compensate for human shortcomings.

6

THE CUP OF FORGIVENESS
Covenant in the Gospels

We have already noted in the Introduction that the word for "covenant" in the New Testament is somewhat unusual. In classical Greek, the typical word for a treaty or covenant was *synthēkē;* the preposition *syn-* ("with") suggests the mutuality connoted by the word. In the Septuagint, however, a different word, *diathēkē*, is used to translate the Hebrew *bᵉrît. Diathēkē* properly means "last will, testament," hence the names Old and New Testaments. There is even a play on these two meanings in one New Testament passage, as we shall see. Most of the New Testament passages are quotations from, or direct allusions to, Hebrew Bible texts. Even when New Testament writers do not directly refer to the Hebrew Bible, the latter clearly informs the message they wish to communicate through the word *covenant*. In short, it is fair to say that the use and meaning of *covenant* in the New Testament is really determined by those of the Hebrew Bible.

The word *diathēkē* occurs thirty-three times in the New Testament. These are distributed among three portions of the New Testament as follows:

83

1. the gospels and Acts: Matthew 26:28; Mark 14:24; Luke 1:72; 22:20; Acts 3:25; 7:8;
2. the letters of Paul: Romans 9:4; 11:27; 1 Corinthians 11:25; 2 Corinthians 3:6, 14; Galations 3:15, 17; 4:24; Ephesians 2:12;
3. the letter to the Hebrews: 7:22; 8:6, 8, 9 (twice), 10; 9:4 (twice), 15 (twice), 16, 17, 20; 10:16, 29; 12:24; 13:20.

There is also one occurrence in the reference to the "ark of the covenant" as part of the vision of the heavenly temple in Revelation 11:19. This illustrates the dependence of the New Testament on the Hebrew Bible for its perspective on "covenant" but does not contribute to that perspective per se. It is the three groupings of texts above that provide the real evidence for the understanding of the New Testament writers. We will treat these three groups in this chapter and the two following.

Supersessionism

Supersessionism is the name for the idea, prevalent among Christians, that the New Testament supersedes or replaces the Hebrew Bible, rendering it obsolete. Hand in hand with this idea goes the related one that Christianity replaces Judaism, which is also considered obsolete. Our consideration of covenant in the New Testament over this chapter and the two that follow is designed in part to address the problem of supersessionism. There are two serious dangers associated with supersessionism. First, it inevitably leads Christians to disregard the Hebrew Bible and the richness of its theology and instruction. Our study will illustrate how the understanding of who God is in Christianity derives principally from the Hebrew Bible and the picture that emerges from the divine-human interaction described in its pages.

Second, supersessionism fosters anti-Semitism. The unspeakable persecutions of Jews over the centuries, including the Holocaust in our own, are not the fault of Christianity. But it is a fact that Christians have collaborated in those persecutions, motivated in part by the belief that Judaism is obsolete and should be destroyed. Our study of covenant will show that Judaism and Christianity hark back to the same covenants. It will suggest that this shared heritage can be one of the primary starting points for dialogue between Jews and Christians about their relationship.

Covenant in the Gospels and Acts

The passages in this category are subdivided into two groups: those that convey Jesus' words at the institution of the Lord's supper and those that occur elsewhere in Luke's writings (the gospel of Luke and the book of Acts).

Luke–Acts

The books of Luke and Acts are really two parts of a single work. Both were written by Luke and addressed to "Theophilus" (Luke 1:3; Acts 1:1). Acts 1:1 refers back to "the first book," that is, the gospel of Luke. The name Theophilus is Greek, and he may have been an official of some sort, as suggested by the title "most excellent" in Luke 1:3. However, the name itself means "lover of God" and could be Luke's way of offering his work to anyone seeking religious truths. As Luke explains in his introduction to Acts (1:1–2), his first book, the gospel, recounts the story of Jesus' life. Volume two, Acts, tells the story of the early church.

Outside of Luke's version of Jesus' institution of the Lord's supper (22:20), which we will treat momentarily, there are three mentions of covenant in Luke's two-volume work. All three are references to Abraham.

Luke 1:72, in the context of the prophecy of Zechariah, father of John the Baptist, after his son's birth, equates God's "holy covenant" with "the oath that he swore to our ancestor Abraham." Similarly, Peter's speech in Acts 3:25 mentions "the covenant that God gave to your ancestors" and then quotes part of the promise to Abraham from the book of Genesis. Acts 7:8, in the context of Stephen's speech, says that God gave Abraham "the covenant of circumcision"—a direct reference to the P account of the Abrahamic covenant in Genesis 17.

All three passages are recitals of the history of God's relationship with Israel in the Hebrew Bible. Hence, all three begin with Abraham, seeing that covenant, rather than the one at Sinai, as the beginning of the relationship. This is not surprising, since it accords with the presentation of the Pentateuch in its final form as edited by P. What is more significant for our present study is that all three of these passages in different ways express the view that later covenants, the one at Sinai and even, for Zechariah, the one with David, are extensions or refinements or renewals of that original covenant. Again, in agreement with P, this series of covenants might be represented by concentric circles. The newer covenant does not abrogate the older one(s) but refines them. Also, all three passages understand covenant, as did P, not as a mutual agreement but unilaterally as a promise or, in the case of the "covenant of circumcision," as a command that is imposed. In short, the understanding of covenant in Luke–Acts is very much in line with the perspective presented by the priestly writer in the finished form of the Pentateuch in the Hebrew Bible.

The Synoptic Problem

According to four New Testament passages, Jesus mentioned "covenant" when he instituted the rite of the Lord's supper at the passover meal (the "Last Supper") on the night of his betrayal. Three of the four are in the synoptic gospels, Matthew, Mark, and Luke (Matt. 26:28; Mark 14:24; Luke 22:20). In order to grasp the reason and significance for this, it is necessary to know something about what is called the "synoptic problem."

The gospels of Matthew, Mark, and Luke are called "synoptic" because they have the same perspective on Jesus in the sense that they follow a similar order of events and have a great deal of material in common. In contrast, the fourth gospel, John, follows an entirely different order of events and has very little material in common with the three synoptics. The synoptic problem is simply the matter of trying to explain why this is so. That is, it raises the question as to why the first three gospels are both similar and different. Why do they follow the same basic outline and share many episodes and yet at the same time have distinctive features and content that set them apart from one another?

The most widely accepted explanation for the synoptic problem is what is called the "two document hypothesis." It can be diagrammed as follows:

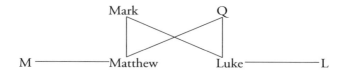

According to this theory, the similarities between the synoptics exist because both Matthew and Luke used Mark as the basis for their gospels. (Note that Luke's introduction in 1:1–4 says that he was aware of other "orderly accounts" about Jesus and that he did "research" by "investigating everything carefully" before writing his own "orderly account.") In addition, the theory postulates a second source document known as "Q" (for German *Quelle,* meaning "source"). The material common to Matthew and Luke but absent from Mark— mostly sayings of Jesus—is accounted for by recourse to Q. Then, Matthew and Luke had their own sources of information—not necessarily written, but oral traditions and the like—from which the material peculiar to each of them came.

Through comparison of the three gospels, scholars isolate what appear to be the particular interests of each author. This process is known as redaction criticism, because scholars seek to determine how each writer edited or redacted the story of Jesus in order to incorporate his own interests and concerns for the Christian community that was his primary audience.[1] Thus, Matthew is generally thought to have written to a Jewish Christian audience, Mark to Romans, and Luke to Greeks. We will see examples later in this chapter of how concern for these different audiences has influenced the telling of the story of Jesus.

Institution of the Lord's Supper

In addition to the three synoptic accounts of the institution of the Lord's supper, there is a fourth in 1 Corinthians 11:25, which must be treated here even though it was written by Paul. All four passages are parallel and describe the same event. It is the only occasion when Jesus is quoted as using the word *covenant.*

Jesus mentions the covenant in all four passages in the context of his reference to the cup of wine as the symbol of his shed blood.

Matt. 26:28	Mark 14:24	Luke 22:20	1 Cor. 11:25
For this is my blood of the covenant which for many is poured out for the forgiveness of sins.	This is my blood of the covenant which is poured out for many.	This cup is the new covenant in my blood which for you is poured out.	This cup is the new covenant in my blood.

---

[1]See Gail P. C. Streete, "Redaction Criticism," in Steven L. McKenzie and Stephen R. Haynes, eds., *To Each Its Own Meaning: Biblical Criticisms and Their Interpretation,* rev. ed. (Louisville, Ky.: Westminster John Knox Press, 1999), 105–21.

Comparison of these four texts indicates that there were two versions of this saying. In light of the two document hypothesis, one version of Jesus' saying probably read, "This is my blood of the covenant which is poured out for many." This is the reading of Mark, which is preserved also in Matthew, though with the addition of the phrase "for the forgiveness of sins." The other version is that of 1 Corinthians 11:25, "This cup is the new covenant in my blood." Luke has this second version but has apparently added "which for you is poured out" based on Mark. What is most important about these two versions for our present purposes is that the one in Mark and Matthew refers to the "covenant," while Luke and 1 Corinthians 11:25 have the "new covenant."

It is difficult to say which of the versions is the older or more original. The gospels, though the first books in the New Testament, were not the first to be written. First Corinthians was written before any of the gospels, so its version of this saying may be the oldest. Another argument in favor of this position is that the saying about the wine in Mark, "This is my blood," matches the one about the bread, "This is my body," and may have been assimilated to it, while the two sayings differ in 1 Corinthians 11:23–25. On the other hand, the fact that Matthew and Mark do not refer to the *new* covenant is remarkable and strongly suggests that theirs is the more original version. It is easy to see how the word *new* could have been introduced into this saying by Christians, who identified their faith as the new covenant. But it is unlikely that the word *new*, if original to the saying, would have been omitted. In fact, there are some manuscripts of Matthew and Mark that contain the word *new* in their version of this saying, but there are no manuscripts of Luke or 1 Corinthians that omit the word *new* from theirs. Finally, the phrase "blood of the covenant" is a quotation from Exodus 24:8, and it seems clear that Jesus is drawing an analogy here between sacrifice and the covenant-making ceremony described in Exodus. Thus, Jesus himself probably never actually spoke of a "new covenant." Nevertheless, the early church clearly understood his words along those lines. So we shall have to explore the implications of the new covenant and how it relates to the previous covenant(s) in the course of this chapter.

Jesus' saying about the Lord's supper, whatever its original form, is filled with allusions to the Hebrew Bible. The most direct allusion, as mentioned, is to Exodus 24:8, in which Moses "pours out" upon the people of Israel "the blood of the covenant" from sacrifices made after the people promise to keep the stipulations of the book of the covenant. Jesus' blood and sacrifice are the means through which the (new) covenant between God and the people is ratified. The further analogy with the passover lamb (Exod. 12:3–13) is unavoidable given the setting upon which Jesus institutes the Lord's supper. The blood of the lamb is the mark of salvation that protects those who have it from death. The expression "for many" in Mark recalls the statement in Isaiah 53:12 that the servant bore the sins "of many." Jesus takes on the role of the Suffering Servant who died vicariously, that is, in place of those who justly deserved punishment. Finally, the new covenant in Luke 22:20 and 1 Corinthians 11:25 brings to mind Jeremiah 31's prophecy of a new covenant, which the early church (and the church ever since) saw as fulfilled in Christianity.

The question that must occupy much of our time in this chapter is, What exactly is meant by the "new covenant" in the New Testament? Is it a brand-new agreement or relationship that renders the old one(s) obsolete, or is it rather an extension or renewal of previous covenants? The answer to this question must decidedly be the latter; the "new covenant" is a renewed covenant, not a completely new one. We can draw this conclusion on several grounds. In the first place, there is the series of covenants in the Hebrew Bible that we have examined in previous chapters—none a replacement of the earlier one(s) but each a refinement or extension. In the present set of texts about Jesus' institution of the Lord's supper, the allusions to various Hebrew Bible passages indicate that this saying continues and participates in the ancient Israelite tradition. Moreover, the other sermons and sayings of Jesus in the gospels reflect the same continuation. We shall now turn to some of these.

The Sermon on the Mount (Matthew 5—7)

The gospel of Matthew especially portrays Jesus as the fulfillment of Hebrew Bible prophecy and expectation. This is apparent from a glance at the "infancy narrative" in the first two chapters of Matthew. These chapters are full of quotations from the Hebrew Bible, and Matthew frequently says that a certain episode in Jesus' infancy fulfilled the words spoken by a prophet in the Hebrew Bible.

It is important to understand that Matthew is employing a kind of interpretation common in his day that related texts or sayings to each other without any concern for those texts' original settings. A good example is Matthew 2:15. Matthew tells how Joseph, acting upon an angelic warning, took Mary and Jesus to Egypt in order to escape from Herod. In verse 15, Matthew says this flight was the fulfillment of a prophecy from Hosea 11:1: "Out of Egypt have I called my son." A glance at Hosea in the Hebrew Bible reveals that this verse originally had nothing to do with Jesus. The complete verse reads: "When Israel was a child I loved him, and out of Egypt I called my son." It employs the analogy of a father-son relationship for that of Yahweh and Israel. The nation of Israel is God's son, whom he brought out of Egypt. The reference is obviously to the exodus. Matthew, however, has "reinterpreted" Hosea 11:1 as a prophecy of Jesus. Again, this kind of interpretation was not unusual in Matthew's day. He uses it here to make a point for his Jewish Christian audience. Jesus was the Messiah, the fulfillment of the expectations of the Hebrew Bible and the Jewish people. The relevance of Matthew's point for our study of covenant lies in the fact that Jesus was fully immersed in the stream of Jewish tradition with its series of covenants between God and God's people.

In chapters 5—7, Matthew presents Jesus' famous "Sermon on the Mount." It is no accident that Matthew is the only one of the gospels to recount the Sermon on the Mount. Luke 6 does contain parallels to some of the sayings in Matthew's sermon. But Luke's version is not nearly as extensive as Matthew's, and in Luke this discourse takes place on a plain, a "level place" (Luke 6:17). This seemingly minor difference is significant. Matthew presents Jesus in the role of a lawgiver like Moses. He delivers the Sermon on the Mount in the same way that Moses went up to Mount Sinai (or Horeb) to receive the law from God. As this parallel suggests, the Sermon on the Mount is a sort of "new law" (or better, "new instruction") to be observed by Christians, comparable to the role of the law of Moses in the Hebrew Bible. The Beatitudes (nine of them in all, plus the imperative "Rejoice" in Matt. 5:12) resemble the Ten Commandments, each at the beginning of their respective bodies of law or instruction. In fact, the gospel of Matthew is organized around five discourses, of which the Sermon on the Mount is the first. The other four are: the commissioning of the twelve disciples in chapter 10, the parables of the kingdom in chapter 13, the teachings about discipleship in chapter 18, and the warning about the end in chapters 24—25. The five discourses match the five books of Moses in the Pentateuch or Torah.

A careful reading of the Sermon on the Mount shows that the "new" instruction of Jesus is really not that much different from that of Moses. In Matthew 5:17, Jesus puts it succinctly, "Do not think that I have come to abolish the law or the prophets; I have come not to abolish but to fulfill" (NRSV). "The law and the prophets" is short-hand for the Hebrew Bible, which is divided into three sections: Law (Torah), Prophets, and Writings. Jesus says he came to fulfill the Law and the Prophets (and, we might add, "its covenants") not by abolishing them or rendering them obsolete, but by bringing out their fullest intended meanings. This is precisely what he does in the rest of the Sermon on the Mount, especially in chapter 5.

Beginning in 5:21, Jesus quotes from the Mosaic law, particularly, but not exclusively, from the Ten Commandments. Typically he says, "You have heard that it was said to those of ancient times...but I say to you..." In the light of his preface to this series of teachings in verse 17, it is apparent that what he is doing is not changing the Mosaic commandments but explaining their real intent. Jesus deals here specifically with the commandments from the Decalogue against murder (vv. 21–26) and adultery (vv. 27–32), and then with those from elsewhere in the law against swearing falsely (vv. 33–37), vengeance (vv. 38–42), and love of the neighbor (vv. 43–48). In all cases he goes beyond the letter of the law to its spirit or intent. Thus, the command was "Thou shalt not kill," but the source of the problem behind murder is anger and hatred. It is those internal feelings that the law was meant to address. Similarly, "Thou shalt not commit adultery" really includes lust, for it is in the heart that the sin begins. In both of these examples, it is not the overt act but the intent of a person's heart that is Jesus' focus and that he says was the real meaning of the law. Jesus' teaching in these two examples, then, is in line with the prophecy of the new covenant in Jeremiah 31 where the law is envisioned as being inscribed on the heart. "It [the new covenant] is everlasting not for the purpose of negating the perpetuity which belongs essentially to the covenant grace exemplified in the older covenants but because it brings that grace to its fullest exhibition and bestowal."[2]

---

[2]J. Murray, "Covenant," in J. D. Douglas, ed., *The New Bible Dictionary* (Grand Rapids, Mich.: Eerdmans, 1967), 267.

The Greatest Commandment

The three synoptic gospels have in common the account of Jesus' response to a question about the greatest commandment, as illustrated in the following table.[3]

Matthew 22:34–40	Mark 12:28–31	Luke 10:25–28
When the Pharisees heard that he had silenced the Sadducees, they gathered together, and one of [the Pharisees], a lawyer, asked him a question to test him. "Teacher, which commandment in the law is the greatest?" He said to him, "You shall love the Lord your God with all your heart, and with all your soul, and with all your mind. This is the greatest and first commandment.	One of the scribes came near and heard them disputing with one another, and seeing that he answered them well, he asked him, "Which commandment is the first of all?" Jesus answered, "The first is, 'Hear, O Israel: the Lord our God, the Lord is one; you shall love the Lord your God with all your heart, and with all your soul, and with all your mind, and with all your strength.'	Just then a lawyer stood up to test him. He said, "Teacher, what must I do to inherit eternal life?" He said to him, "What is written in the law? What do you read there?" He answered, "You shall love the Lord your God with all your heart, and with all your soul, and with all your strength, and with all your mind;
And a second is like it: 'You shall love your neighbor as yourself.' On these two commandments hang all the law and the prophets."	The second is this, 'You shall love your neighbor as yourself.' There is no other commandment greater than these."	and your neighbor as yourself." And he said to him, "You have given the right answer; do this, and you will live."

All three synoptic gospels agree in the basic content of these two commandments. But the settings of this episode are different in all three. Matthew and Luke refer to the questioner as a lawyer who was trying to test Jesus, while Mark says he was a scribe and does not mention testing. Matthew and Mark both have the questioner ask about the first commandment and have Jesus answer the question

---

[3]The translations are from the NRSV, except for Luke's version, where I have made minor changes to reflect the Greek more literally.

directly. In Luke, the man asks how to attain eternal life and then answers his own question when Jesus returns it to him. Matthew and Mark also specifically say that love for the neighbor is the second commandment, while Luke treats the love for God and love for the neighbor as part of the same command.

Our concern here is not to try to reconstruct the original wording of this conversation but to consider the implications of all three passages for the understanding of covenant. It is clear in all three versions that these two commandments are the "first" (and "second") or "greatest" in terms of importance. Matthew and Luke describe them as the epitome of the law. Matthew says that the law and the prophets (again, shorthand for the entire Hebrew Bible) hangs on these two commandments. In Luke, the lawyer cites these two commandments as a way of summing up the meaning of the law. The first commandment, the love for God, is found in the Hebrew Bible in Deuteronomy 6:4: "Hear, O Israel: Yahweh is our God; Yahweh is one; you shall love the Yahweh your God with all your heart, and with all your soul, and with all your mind, and with all your strength."[4] Mark's citation is nearly verbatim. The Deuteronomy text is also known as the *Shema'* ("Hear!"). It is the essential confession of Judaism that is still recited in synagogues today. By answering the question in this way, Jesus pronounces the chief religious obligation of Christians to be the same as that of ancient Israel and of Jews. In Luke's version the lawyer probably took pride in his citation of the national confession; he seems to have seen it as what set Israel apart from the nations or Gentiles and therefore as a way of excluding non-Jews. He was undoubtedly hoping to trap and embarrass Jesus by asking him to explain who qualified as his neighbor. Jesus avoided the trap by telling the story of the good Samaritan (Luke 10:29–37). It must have galled the lawyer that the hero of the story was a Samaritan, since Jews typically hated Samaritans, regarding them as half-breeds and apostates. At the end of the story when Jesus asked the lawyer who proved to be a neighbor, the lawyer would not even say "Samaritan" but replied instead with a circumlocution, "The one who showed him mercy." Even more galling was Jesus' instruction to emulate the Samaritan (v. 37).

---

[4]Mark 12:28–30. Compare Matthew 22:36–37; Luke 10:25–28. For a discussion of the meaning of this confession see the next chapter.

As we saw in the chapter on Deuteronomy, the command to love God borrows from the language of ancient Near Eastern treaties. Those who "love" the suzerain keep the stipulations of the covenant with him; those who "hate" him do not. (Compare 2 Sam. 19:7, where Joab accuses David of loving those who hate him and hating those who love him because he is more distraught over the death of his rebellious son Absalom than he is grateful to the loyal servants who fought for him.) The love for God is a covenant obligation. It can be commanded because it is not an emotional response. It is rather obedience to the divine commands. Thus, Christianity shares the same covenant as Judaism. The epitome of the law, the epitome of Judaism, is also the epitome of Christianity. The prime directive under the Mosaic covenant is the same under Jesus—love God with all your being by obeying his commands.

Jesus adds that the second greatest commandment is similar: "You shall love your neighbor as yourself." It is true that in the Hebrew Bible, one's neighbor was defined as a fellow Israelite. But Jesus explains the law's true intent. The parable of the good Samaritan in Luke (10:29–37) is not a "nice story"; it is full of barbs that were directed against the ethnic and religious prejudice of the lawyer and his cronies.[5] At the same time, it makes clear that God is concerned for all people without regard for national or ethnic boundaries. The neighbor can be anyone. This is a not a principle unique to Christianity. Jews would also endorse it. Indeed, the point of Jesus' teaching in this instance, as in the Sermon on the Mount, is that the true intent of the law in the Hebrew Bible was love for everyone.

Conclusions

The passages we have treated in this chapter have in common that they see the "new" covenant of Christianity very much in the line and heritage of the covenants in the Hebrew Bible. This accords well with the depiction of covenant by both the priestly writer and the Deuteronomistic historian in the Hebrew Bible.

It is not certain that Jesus ever used the expression "new covenant." In instituting the Lord's supper at his last meal with the disciples, he made allusions to ideas and practices in Judaism that were

---

[5]See my treatment of the parable in Steven L. McKenzie, *All God's Children: A Biblical Critique of Racism* (Louisville, Ky.: Westminster John Knox Press, 1997), 93–97.

based on those of ancient Israel. Certainly, what Jesus was about to do—suffer and die for the forgiveness of sins for all of his followers—was new in many ways. But it was also incomprehensible apart from the background of God's dealings with Israel over the previous millennium or two. What is more, in his teachings Jesus clearly followed the Hebrew Bible. He stated explicitly that he had not come to annul it or its covenants, but to bring them to their full intent. He fully endorsed the main principles of the Hebrew Bible that epitomized its message of love for God and for fellow humans. His teachings, such as those in the Sermon on the Mount, that might be perceived as changes to the law really sought to elucidate the law's true intent. The instruction expounded by Jesus did not replace that given by Moses, but in one sense returned to it and clarified it.

7

HEIRS THROUGH FAITH
Covenant in Paul

Besides 1 Corinthians 11:25, treated in the last chapter, the term *covenant* (*diathēkē*) occurs only eight times in the letters ascribed to Paul in the New Testament (Rom. 9:4; 11:27; 2 Cor. 3:6, 14; Gal. 3:15, 17; 4:24; Eph. 2:12). Hence, the topic of covenant does not figure significantly in most modern discussions of Paul's writings. Nevertheless, it can be seen as an important element of his theology.[1] The occurrences of the term listed above fall within five distinct passages. In approximate order of composition, these are: Galatians 3; 4:21–31; 2 Corinthians 3; Romans 9—11; and Ephesians 2.[2]

---

[1]As has been argued in detail by Paul Shang-Hsin Liao, "The Place of Covenant in the Theology of the Apostle Paul," unpublished Ph.D. dissertation, Hartford Seminary, 1973. So also Larry Kreitzer, *2 Corinthians* (NTG; Sheffield: Sheffield Academic Press, 1976), 61–62.

[2]These are the passages treated by Liao, who also includes Romans 4:1–25. We will cite Romans 4:1–25 in the course of our treatment of the other passages but have omitted it from special consideration because it does not contain the word *covenant*.

The Epistle to the Galatians

Galatians was one of Paul's earliest epistles. It was written in the early 50s C.E. and was directed to Christians in central Asia Minor or Anatolia (modern Turkey).[3] In it Paul defends himself and his gospel against the onslaught of the "Judaizers." These were Jewish Christians who taught that Gentiles had to undergo circumcision before they could become Christians. Put another way, the Judaizers required Gentiles to be proselytes to Judaism before they could convert to Christianity. Paul held that circumcision was unnecessary for salvation. In the course of his argument he discusses the question of Christians and Jewish law and touches on the relationship of Christianity to the covenants of the Hebrew Bible, which is of prime interest to us.

The intensity of Paul's feelings on these matters is suggested by the beginning of the epistle. He omits his usual thanksgivings and launches directly into his defense with an expression of dismay that the Galatians have so quickly turned to a "different gospel" from the one he proclaimed to them (1:6–7). His language is the strongest possible, as he damns those who have been preaching this "different gospel" (1:8–9). He then turns to his own personal religious history.

The autobiographical information that Paul provides in Galatians 1—2 is extremely important for an understanding of the early history of Christianity. More important for our present concerns, however, is the background that it furnishes to Paul's theology, especially his understanding of covenant. Raised in Judaism, Paul had persecuted the church until he became a convert as the result of a personal revelation of Jesus (Gal. 1:13–24; cf. Acts 9). His zealousness as a Jew (1:14) may already have convinced him of the impossibility of keeping the entire law (cf. Gal. 5:3). His mission to the Gentiles following his conversion showed him that justification was not to be achieved by works of the law but by faith (Gal. 2:16; cf. Rom. 4), and that is the focus of his argument in Galatians 3—4, which is the heart of the book and which contains the references to covenant.

---

[3]For discussions of introductory matters see Hans Dieter Betz, "Galatians," *ABD* 2:872–74; and Sam K. Williams, *Galatians,* ANTC (Nashville: Abingdon Press, 1997), 15–32.

Galatians 3

In the third chapter, Paul points to Abraham, who "believed God, and it was reckoned to him as righteousness" (Gal. 3:6; Gen. 15:6). Hence, the real descendants of Abraham are those who believe, which includes Gentiles (3:7–9). Justification, therefore, occurs by faith, not by the law (3:11–12).

Beginning in verse 15, Paul uses a legal analogy that also plays on the different nuances of the Greek word *diathēkē*. The first use of the word in verse 15 is translated "will" or "testament" in most English versions. Paul's point is that a will or testament cannot be changed once it has been ratified following the death of the testator. So it is, he says, with the covenant of God with Abraham. God's *diathēkē* to Abraham (and through him to Gentiles, see v. 29) of justification through faith is not nullified by the later *diathēkē* introducing the law for Abraham's other heirs, the Jews (v. 17). Again this is similar to the notion in the Hebrew Bible that a "new" covenant does not render a previous one obsolete. "The law, which came four hundred thirty years later, does not annul a covenant previously ratified by God, so as to nullify the promise" (v. 17, NRSV). The law, Paul goes on to say in verses 19–29, was like a "disciplinarian" (v. 24). The word (*paidagogos*) refers to a household position in the Greek world. The *paidagogos* was responsible for accompanying children to and from school and other activities in order to protect them. The law, therefore, in this analogy served to keep sin at bay by means of rules and regulations until its completion in faith—the placing of the law, so to speak, upon the heart as in Jeremiah 31.

Paul's argument implies that Christians, as the true descendants of Abraham and the heirs to the promises, are also the heirs to the covenant made to him. The question immediately arises as to the disposition of the Sinai covenant. Paul contends that Christians are not required to keep the laws given to Moses on Sinai. But he does not mention the Mosaic covenant. Does the covenant in Christ nullify the covenant under Moses itself? This is a very difficult question and one that Paul speaks to in other epistles in addition to Galatians, as we shall see. In fact, it is worth observing here that because Paul addresses specific situations in different churches, it is not easy to distinguish a single clear answer to the question. The passage referring to covenant in the next chapter of Galatians does deal with the issue, but it also illustrates the difficulty with trying to discern Paul's position.

Galatians 4:21–31

Paul continues the same line of thought into the next chapter of Galatians. He tells his Gentile readers that they are like heirs who have come of age or slaves who have been freed to receive the promised inheritance (4:1–7). In 4:21–31 he makes another analogy, even waxing allegorical. The two women in the Abraham story, he says, are two covenants. Hagar is the covenant of flesh at Sinai; Sarah is the covenant of spirit in Christ. Hagar represents enslavement to the law; Sarah represents freedom. The analogy again recalls Jeremiah's "new covenant," which is to be inscribed on the heart.

Paul's concern is to address the situation of his readers, whom he considers the heirs of the spiritual covenant, that is, Christianity; he does not tell what happens to the fleshly covenant, that is, Sinai and Judaism. While Paul clearly sees the covenant in Christ as superior, he still does not speak of the nullification or obsolescence of the one at Sinai. To be sure, in 4:30 he quotes from Genesis 21: "Cast out the slave and her son, for the son of the slave shall not share the inheritance with the son of the free woman." And in the analogy, Hagar and Ishmael were driven out from Abraham and Sarah (Gal. 4:30; Gen. 21:10). But both women continued to live; their heirs grew up next to each other; and God made of Hagar's descendants a great nation according to promise just as he did of Sarah's (Gen. 16:10; 21:20–21). So the question about the status of the Sinai covenant and its adherents remains. Is this covenant still in effect, or has it been abrogated? Are the Jews still God's chosen people? As suggested above, this is a topic to which Paul would return in later correspondence.

In the remainder of Galatians, Paul moves into a discussion of the ethical implications of freedom in Christ. While he does not mention covenant again, there is one more verse that has important implications for our consideration of covenant in the New Testament. The verse is 5:14: "For the whole law is summed up in a single commandment, 'You shall love your neighbor as yourself'" (NRSV). The word translated "summed up" by the NRSV can also be rendered "fulfilled" or even "accomplished." This statement is very similar to the passage shared by the synoptic gospels about the greatest and second greatest commandment (see chapter 6). Matthew's statement in

22:40 is especially similar: "On these two commandments hang all the law and the prophets" (NRSV). For Paul, as for Jesus, the real intent of the law is love. It is a quality that transcends boundaries of race, ethnicity, and even religion. It is the essence shared by both the Sinai covenant and the new covenant under Christ, and other matters regarding ritual practice and dogma pale by comparison.

2 Corinthians

Second Corinthians is one of the most challenging books in the New Testament for discerning its historical setting. Fortunately, there is a wealth of recent scholarship on the book for readers who may wish to explore it in detail.[4] Most New Testament scholars regard 2 Corinthians as a collection of portions from several originally independent letters written to the church at Corinth somewhere around 55 C.E. addressing different problems there. However, this reconstruction of the book's origin is not essential for understanding its references to covenant, which are our main concern here.

2 Corinthians 3:6

The portion of 2 Corinthians that concerns us at present begins in 2:14. As in Galatians, Paul here offers a defense of his ministry against accusations from unnamed opponents, who may have been Judaizers. Hence, he says in 2:17 that he and those with him are sincere ministers of God's word and not peddlers like so many others (i.e., his opponents). His commission, he states, comes from God. He asks in 3:1–3 whether he needs a letter of recommendation in order for the Corinthians to heed his message and then replies that they themselves are his letter of recommendation, written on tablets of human (lit. "fleshly") hearts, because he had worked among them. Perhaps it was his familiarity with Jeremiah 31, to which he would allude in verse 6, that led Paul to use the metaphor of writing on the heart here.

---

[4]One good place to begin is Hans Dieter Betz, "Corinthians, Second Epistle to the," *ABD* 1:1148–54. Another is Larry Kreitzer, *2 Corinthians,* cited above. There are several recent commentaries that have been published since Betz's article or that are not mentioned in its bibliography (though some are referred to in the text of the article): Victor Paul Furnish, *II Corinthians,* AB 32A (Garden City, N.Y.: Doubleday, 1984); Ralph P. Martin, *2 Corinthians,* WBC 40 (Waco, Tex.: Word, 1986); Margaret E. Thrall, *The Second Epistle to the Corinthians,* vol. 1, *Introduction and Commentary on II Corinthians I–VII,* ICC (Edinburgh: T. & T. Clark, 1994).

As part of his defense, Paul asserts in 3:6 that God has made him and his companions ministers of a "new covenant." This is the only reference in Paul's writings to the "new covenant" outside of his account of Jesus' institution of the Lord's supper in 1 Corinthians 11:25. The language of a new covenant is obviously borrowed in part from Jeremiah 31. But Paul is drawing a different contrast from that in Jeremiah. The contrast Paul draws is not between the "old" covenant under Moses on Sinai and the "new" covenant under Christ. It is rather a contrast between two different understandings of the new covenant.[5] The Greek literally reads, "who qualified us to be ministers of the new covenant not of the letter but of the spirit." Grammatically, "not of the letter but of the spirit" modifies "new covenant." Paul's Judaizing opponents claimed to be ministers of the new covenant. They may well have quoted from Jeremiah 31. But Paul says they have misunderstood the nature of the new covenant by their insistence on keeping the law of Moses. The new covenant is spiritual and lifegiving; it is not "of the letter," which kills.

Paul's words here fit very well with Jeremiah 31 and with descriptions of the "new covenant" in the gospels. He neither says nor implies that the old covenant is obsolete. Rather, in Christ it is made spiritual. This accords with Jeremiah's message that the new covenant would be inscribed on the heart. The new covenant is the old covenant refurbished and internalized.

2 Corinthians 3:7–18

These verses further elaborate on the contrast between spirit and letter that Paul introduced in verse 6. It is clear here that the letter is identified with the law of Moses. The contrast is threefold. Since the letter kills, the "dispensation" (NRSV; the Greek literally means "ministry") under Moses is designated the dispensation of death (3:7). It is important to note that Paul does not use the term *covenant*. Paul does not argue that the "old" and "new" covenants are opposed or that the "new" covenant has nullified the "old" one. When the law was given it was accompanied by such brightness that the people of Israel could not bear to gaze on Moses' face. Here Paul draws on the story in

---

[5]See Jerome Murphy-O'Connor, *The Theology of the Second Letter to the Corinthians* (Cambridge: Cambridge University Press, 1991), 32–33. See esp. p. 33, n. 24, where Murphy-O'Connor cites Furnish, *II Corinthians*, 199.

Exodus 34:29–35. The first contrast, therefore, relates to splendor. If the first ministry—that of the letter, which kills—came with such splendor, the ministry of the spirit must be all the more resplendent (vv. 8–9). The second contrast is that of condemnation as opposed to righteousness (v. 9). Paul does not here explain these terms, but we may discern what he means based on his other writings, in particular what we have already examined in Galatians. The law inevitably led to condemnation because it was impossible to keep completely, but the new covenant brings justification through faith in Christ. The new ministry, therefore, accomplishes what the law never could. The third contrast is between the fading nature of the written dispensation (v. 8) and the permanence of the new one (v. 11).

It must be remembered in all of this that Paul's argumentation is directed against his opponents. It is "*not* intended as a polemic against Judaism as a whole."[6] If Judaizers, the opponents would be attempting to hold on to the regulations of the written law of Moses. At any rate, the question behind the contrasts drawn by Paul is, Why cling to the old law when something so much better is available in Christ? For the Judaizers and perhaps others, Moses was the principal religious figure. Paul, therefore, takes on Moses not to demean him or his work, but to point out that the "ministry" under him, though necessary for its era, was imperfect and that blindly following him makes no sense in light of the availability of something far superior.[7] In verses 12–18 Paul further exploits the story in Exodus 34:29–35. In contrast to Moses, who had to veil his face because of its brightness, Paul and his companions have confidence as ministers of the new covenant to be open and bold in their ministry. Paul's ministry is far superior to those who still claim to represent Moses. Paul also implies that he and those with him are open and honest, in contrast to his opponents, who are underhanded.

In verse 14 Paul shifts the meaning that he attributes to Moses as Moses becomes a metaphor for the law. The term "old covenant" in verse 14 obviously refers to the Torah in the Hebrew Bible. In verse 15 Paul refers to this same section of scripture not as the law or books of Moses, but simply as Moses. Again, this may be because of the special status his opponents ascribe to Moses and the use they have

---

[6]Kreitzer, *2 Corinthians*, 57.

[7]See Murphy-O'Conner, *Theology of the Second Letter to the Corinthians*, 36–37.

made of Moses to discredit Paul and his ministry. However, Paul may also continue this metaphor in order to introduce a different image for the veil. It has been suggested that the veil in verse 16 refers to the practice of covering the Torah scroll in a synagogue with a piece of cloth and then removing the cloth when the scroll was read. The person who turns to Christ has the veil removed and is able to view the real glory that was inherent already in the Mosaic covenant (vv. 16–18). If this understanding is correct, what Paul is actually saying is that the new covenant clarifies the old and allows one to get at its real message. This is very much like Jesus' statement in Matthew that he came not to abolish the law but to bring it to completion and show its true intent.

The Epistle to the Romans

Paul wrote Romans some time in the latter half of the 50s C.E. It was probably intended as an encyclical to be circulated among the various house churches in Rome. While the book has often been taken as Paul's systematic exposition of his theology, it is better understood, like his other letters, as addressing specific circumstances within the Roman church.[8]

Unlike the other churches to which Paul wrote, he had not founded the one in Rome. He wanted to visit the Roman Christians and to preach among them but had so far been prevented from doing so (1:9–13; 15:22). He wrote to them in part to introduce himself and to seek their support in his planned journey to Spain (15:24–28). But he also sought to address problems in the church at Rome about which he had learned. In particular, there were divisions, apparently between Jewish and Gentile Christians and churches. These divisions may have been occasioned in part by the edict of Claudius in 49 C.E. expelling the Jews from Rome. The expulsion is reported by the Roman historian Suetonius (ca. 120 C.E.), who says that it occurred because of a certain "Chrestus." This is probably a mistake for "Christ," and it seems likely that the disturbances that led to the expulsion were brought on by disagreements between Jews and Jewish Christians over whether Jesus was the Messiah or Christ. By the time Paul wrote his epistle, the Jews had been allowed to return. But

---

[8]See especially Joseph A. Fitzmyer, *Romans, AB* 33 (New York: Doubleday, 1993), 68–80.

in the meantime the Gentile church had grown, and tensions between them and the returning Jews naturally arose. Some of these tensions had to do with accommodations to government or society against which one group (probably the Jews) felt scruples of conscience (Rom. 13—14). Paul sought to soothe these tensions and to cultivate sensitivity on the part of the different groups to each other and unity within the body of Christ (Rom. 12). It was in this context that Paul addressed the question of the relationship of God to the Jews, particularly those who did not accept Christ, now that the Christian era had dawned (Rom. 9—11). It is here that his two references to covenant are found.

Romans 9—11

These chapters are a distinct section within the epistle to the Romans. Some have even proposed that they contain a sermon that Paul preached at a synagogue and then incorporated into the letter.[9] Paul does seem at pains to defend himself against the charge that he has abandoned his own people, the Jews, in his promotion of Christianity, though this concern can be understood in the light of the Jewish/Gentile division that Paul is trying to address in the church at Rome. Paul vehemently denies that he has abandoned his people, expressing his great concern for them and even wishing he could sacrifice himself on their behalf (9:3).

It is in this context that he mentions "the covenants" as attributes of Israel and Judaism. There is some uncertainty about the reading at this point, with some manuscripts reading the plural and others the singular. The singular would refer, of course, to the Sinai covenant under Moses. But if the plural is original, it does not contradict the point we have made in earlier chapters about later covenants being renewals or refurbishings of earlier ones. Rather, Paul recognizes the series of covenants described in the Hebrew Bible, all of which collectively defined who Israel was and what it meant to be Jewish.

In the rest of chapter 9, Paul goes on to say that the unbelief of the Jews does not signify the failure of God's promises (v. 6). As in Galatians, he argues that true Israelites are not those who are physically descended from Abraham, but those who share Abraham's faith.

[9]Richard A. Batey, *The Letter of Paul to the Romans* (The Living Word Commentary; Austin, Tex.: Sweet, 1969), 120.

"It is not the children of the flesh who are the children of God, but the children of the promise are reckoned as descendants" (9:8). This statement reviews a point that Paul has already argued at length in Romans 4. God's will is sovereign when it comes to election; humans cannot question him, but they can be assured that his choices are grounded in his mercy (9:6–23). This includes God's choice at present of the Gentiles, while the Jews have "stumbled" over Christ and only a remnant of them believe in him; this situation was foreseen in the Old Testament (9:24–33).

In chapter 10, Paul states that Jews have a zeal for God, but that it is unenlightened because they still try to establish their own righteousness through the law (something that is impossible to do) instead of through Christ, who is the end of the law (10:4). The word *end* (*telos*) here does not mean termination or conclusion, but goal or purpose. Again, this is similar to other texts in the New Testament that we have already treated, since the claim is that Christ brings the law to its full intent and meaning. Thus, in 10:5–14, Paul contends, again similar to Galatians, that the principle of justification by faith for all people was laid down in the Hebrew Scriptures. Nevertheless, Israel has not obeyed the preaching of the gospel (10:14–21).

Paul then asks at the beginning of chapter 11 whether God has rejected the Jews as his people. His answer? "By no means" (11:1). The rest of the chapter explains that the disbelief that has come upon the Jews is partial and temporary, a part of God's plan designed to provoke the Jews to salvation. This is the "mystery" of God's plan that Paul now reveals to his readers. Of particular interest to us is the analogy in 11:17–24, where he describes Israel as a tree, some of whose branches are broken off and other branches (Gentiles) grafted on. The tree may be described as representing God's covenant with Israel, and this seems to be Paul's definition in verse 27, where he quotes from Isaiah 59:21, "This is my covenant with them." The relationship that Christians have with God, in other words, is not a brand-new covenant, but one that grafts them onto the covenant of God with Israel. Thus, "the gifts and the calling of God are irrevocable" (11:29), and "all Israel will be saved" (11:26).

It is difficult to know what to make of these statements. Is Paul claiming eternal salvation for Jews who do not believe in Christ? Or is he saying that all Jews will eventually come to believe in Christ? Or does "all Israel" allude to his statements in chapter 9 and refer to all who believe as "true" Israel, as opposed to those who are Jewish by birth? In the light of the context of all of Paul's writings, the second option seems most likely. That is, Paul apparently believed that all Jews would one day come to accept Christ. What is clearer, however, and more important for our present concerns, is that Paul in this passage is very much in agreement with what he says elsewhere concerning the "new covenant" of Christianity and even with what the gospels say. The "new" covenant in Christ stands in line with the covenants in the Hebrew Bible. It is part of the same tree, not an altogether new stock. This line of previous covenants is not abolished or nullified with the coming of Christianity. Rather, in Christ they reach their climax in terms of their real intent and significance.

Ephesians 2:12

The final reference to covenant in the New Testament epistles attributed to Paul may not actually have been written by him. Most New Testament scholars believe that the writing style of Ephesians as well as its theology vary significantly from those of the unquestionably Pauline books (Romans, 1 and 2 Corinthians, Galatians, Philippians, 1 Thessalonians, Philemon) and conclude that Ephesians was written in Paul's name by an otherwise anonymous author, a literary practice that was common in the ancient Greek world. This is a complicated and controversial matter that lies beyond the scope of this book.[10] However it may have been composed, the book of Ephesians is still part of the New Testament and therefore remains important for the study of any theme such as covenant, whether Paul is its author or not.

Ephesians 2:12 is part of an admonition directed to Gentiles reminding them that they were once "aliens from the commonwealth of Israel, and strangers to the covenants of promise." This passage agrees with Romans, then, in pointing out that the Jews were God's chosen people. Instead of the image of a tree, however, Ephesians employs a political metaphor to represent Israel's elect status. The expression "covenants of promise" is also reminiscent of the statement in Romans 9:4 that the "covenants" (plural) belong to Israel. As in Romans, this would appear to refer to the series of covenants from

---

[10]For a detailed review of the arguments see Victor Paul Furnish, "Ephesians, Epistle to the," *ABD* 2:535–42, esp. 539–41.

Abraham on in the Hebrew Bible that are directed toward Israelites and exclude other peoples. It also appears to understand the covenants, including the one at Sinai, as unilateral and promissory rather than mutually agreed upon contracts. But this understanding is not unusual; it appears already in late references to covenant in the Hebrew Bible, as we have seen.

Ephesians 2:13–14 goes on to say that, in Jesus, the wall of separation between Jews and Gentiles has been torn down so that Gentiles also approach God and have salvation. The next verse (v. 15) seems to identify the dividing wall with the Old Testament law, which Gentiles did not know and could not follow. What is striking for our present purposes, though, is the statement in verse 19: "So then you are no longer strangers and aliens, but you are citizens with the saints and also members of the household of God" (NRSV). In Christ, the author says, the Gentiles, who formerly were aliens outside of Israel, have now been made citizens. By the same token, they are no longer "strangers to the covenants of promise" (2:12) but recipients of those covenants. Put another way, this passage says that, in Christ, the Gentiles have become part of the covenantal community of Israel. The Christian community is not an altogether newly constituted one with a brand-new charter, but the continuation of the community of old under the same charter or covenant(s).

Conclusions

What Paul had to say about covenant was shaped largely by his conflicts with the Judaizers and perhaps others. For Paul, Christianity was, in effect, both something new and something old. Paul emphasized that what was new in the Christian era was justification by faith. That is, a person could now be made right before God (i.e., justified) by faith in Christ. One could never achieve justification through the law, because it was impossible to follow the entire law precisely. Hence, it was no longer necessary to try to keep the law, as the Judaizers contended. The Judaizers failed to comprehend the grace of God now available in Christ through faith. Their teaching was oppressive and dangerous because they turned people away from the true freedom offered in Christ. There was freedom in Christ precisely because of the spiritual nature of the relationship. The spiritual relationship with God now available in Christ was far superior to what the physical, "fleshly" demands of the law, such as circumcision, could offer.

At the same time, however, Christianity could never be completely divorced from Judaism. The roots of Christianity ran deep in the Old Testament and in the history of God's relationship with Israel. Christianity was the culmination of that relationship, the fulfillment of the series of promissory covenants going back to Abraham. The purpose of God's relationship with Israel all along had been to reach all peoples. Still, Israel was God's chosen, and Paul held the conviction that the Jews would one day come to believe in Christ.

In addition to its heritage in Israel, Christianity also endorsed the ethical code of the Old Testament. While the "fleshly" regulations of the law were no longer valid, spiritual freedom in Christ was also not a license for immorality (cf. 1 Cor. 5–6; Gal. 5:16–26). The contrast is sometimes drawn between the ethics of the Old Testament or Judaism as a set of written laws and Christianity as principles. But this contrast is misleading, because the laws in the Hebrew Bible are also based on principles. Paul, in accordance with other New Testament writers, emphasized and reinforced these principles when he stated, for instance, that the entire law was summed up in the command to love one's neighbor as oneself. In that sense, Christianity marked not the demise of the Old Testament law, but its culmination. Christian teaching was not something new, but the highlighting of principles that the Hebrew Bible had always espoused.

8

HEAVENLY FORM AND EARTHLY REALITY
Covenant in Hebrews

The book of Hebrews is unique among the writings of the New Testament. Right away it presents the reader with something of a mystery just in trying to determine what kind of literature it represents. It is often referred to as a letter or epistle (NRSV), but it lacks the typical epistolary introduction, which identifies the letter writer and the intended recipient. (Compare the beginnings of the other letters in the New Testament.) Nevertheless, it ends like a letter with personal greetings and references (13:22–25). The possibility that an original epistolary opening was lost is not convincing, because the present beginning of the book is perfectly appropriate rhetorically. By the same token, it is unlikely that the present epistolary conclusion is a later addition, since the final chapter is crucial to the book's message in that it follows up on the call to worship in Hebrews 12:28. Recent treatments of Hebrews, therefore, see it as a homily or a collection of sermons assembled in writing and sent out in letter form.[1] This characterization fits with the author's description of the work as a "word of exhortation" (13:22) and with the contents of the book, which several times offer expositions of texts from the Hebrew Bible. The same expression, "word of exhortation," is used in Acts 13:15 for a speech in the synagogue following the reading of scripture ("law and prophets"). Exposition is also the type of address given by Jesus in the synagogue in Nazareth at the beginning of his ministry (Luke 4:16–21).

The Author of Hebrews

Since there is no epistolary introduction to the book of Hebrews, its author is never identified. The book has traditionally been ascribed to Paul. But this tradition became common only in the third and fourth centuries C.E. Before then, Pauline authorship was rejected by several of the early church leaders.[2] Modern scholars almost universally deny attribution to Paul on stylistic grounds. One recent commentator lists the following five differences between Paul's writings and Hebrews:[3] (1) While the author of Hebrews claims only second-hand acquaintance with Jesus (Heb. 2:3), Paul insisted that he had not received the gospel through human agency, but directly from Christ himself (Gal. 1:11–17). (2) The Greek language and style of Hebrews are polished and smooth—the best in the New Testament, according to some scholars[4]—while Paul's writing style is abrupt and his arguments sometimes hard to follow because of the suddenness with which he shifts topics. (3) The imagery found in Hebrews is more diverse than that employed by Paul. (4) The vocabulary of Hebrews is distinctive and includes more than 150 words not found elsewhere in the New Testament. (5) The theology of Hebrews differs from that of Paul, particularly in its (Hebrews') explanation of Christ's work through analogies drawn from sacrifice and worship in the Hebrew Bible.

---

[1]See Harold W. Attridge, "Hebrews, Epistle to the," *ABD* 3:98; and Victor C. Pfitzner, *Hebrews* (ANTC; Nashville: Abingdon Press, 1997), 20.

[2]See Pfitzner, *Hebrews,* 24–25.

[3]Ibid., 25–26.

[4]Barnabas Lindars, *The Theology of the Letter to the Hebrews* (Cambridge: Cambridge University Press, 1991), 21.

Various other New Testament figures have been proposed as the author of Hebrews. Prominent among these is Apollos, whose Jewish background and familiarity with scripture together with his Hellenistic education and renown as an orator (Acts 18:24) fit well with the nature of the book of Hebrews. However, Apollos is only a possibility, and we must admit that the author of Hebrews is simply unknown.

Audience

We are on firmer ground when it comes to discerning the audience for the book of Hebrews. The title, "to the Hebrews," was added later, and there is no explicit mention anywhere in the book of Jews as the intended audience. Still, the content of the book does seem to presuppose an acquaintance with the Hebrew Bible, so it is not unreasonable to assume that Jewish Christians were its primary audience. This does not mean, though, that this audience lived in Palestine. The next-to-last sentence of the book says, "Those from Italy send you greetings." Apparently, some people who are with the author are sending their greetings home. This statement, therefore, indicates that the letter's destination is Italy, and most likely Rome. This conclusion receives a measure of confirmation from the fact that the first early Christian document to allude to Hebrews is the epistle of 1 Clement, which was written in Rome.

Date and Setting

When it comes to dating the book of Hebrews, we are back in the realm of uncertainty. The upper limit is established by 1 Clement, which appears to know Hebrews, and which was written circa 96 C.E. Some attempt to lower that limit, arguing that the book must have been written before 70 C.E because its discussion of sacrifices presupposes that the temple was still in existence.[5] (The temple was destroyed by the Romans in 70 C.E., making it impossible for Jews to sacrifice there.) This argument is not entirely convincing, because the description of the temple sacrifices in Hebrews is drawn from the Hebrew Bible and not necessarily from the practice of the author's day (see below). Still, the absence of any allusion to the destruction of the temple seems strange if the work was written after 70.

---

[5]Philip Edgcumbe Hughes, "Hebrews, The Letter to the," in Bruce M. Metzger and Michael D. Coogan, eds., *The Oxford Companion to the Bible* (New York: Oxford University Press, 1993), 275.

As for the lower limit of the book, the persecution "in those earlier days" in Hebrews 10:32–34 may refer to the edict of Claudius in 49 C.E. expelling Jews, probably including Jewish Christians, from Rome.[6] Some time has obviously passed since "those earlier days," so a date around 60 seems about right for the lower limit.

There are several clues in chapters 10—13 especially that the audience of the book is beginning to experience some pressure—social, governmental, or both—that challenges their faith. A part of the book's purpose, therefore, is to strengthen its audience in the face of such opposition. The statement in 12:4 that no one in the audience has yet "resisted to the point of shedding your blood" may help further to pinpoint a date. It could not have been written to Christians in Rome after Nero's persecution in 64, when some of them were martyred for their faith. Hence, a date circa 60–64 seems the most likely scenario for the book, though any time between 60 and 90 remains possible.

Structure and Argument

Various plans have been proposed as ways of delineating the structure of the book of Hebrews. For our purposes, the book may be divided into three parts. The first section is 1:1—4:13. Its theme is the word of God, more specifically the superiority of Christ to previous revelations. Thus, while God spoke formerly through prophets, God has now spoken through the Son, who shares God's essence (1:1–3). Christ is superior to angels (1:5—2:18) and to Moses (3:1–6) and Joshua (4:1–10). The section ends as it began, by referring to the word of God, which is sharper than a two-edged sword (4:11–12).

The second and central section is 4:14—10:39. It concerns Christ as the new and superior high priest (picking up on 2:17–18). He is able to sympathize with human weakness because he was human (4:15). He was appointed high priest by God after the order of Melchizedek (5:1–10). Following an exhortation to advance to Christian maturity (chapter 6), the author returns to the topic of Jesus' priesthood in Melchizedek's order (chapter 7). Jesus' appointment, like Melchizedek's, is eternal (7:17), and unlike the Levitical priests, Jesus was sinless (7:26–28). The next two and one-half chapters (8:1—10:18) continue this image of Christ as high priest

---

[6]William L. Lane, *Hebrews 1–8*, (WBC 47A; Dallas: Word, 1991), lviii; lxiii—vi.

and add an exposition of Jeremiah 31:31–34 (Heb. 8:8–12). The new covenant under Christ's priesthood is superior to the old because Christ offered himself once for all for the forgiveness of sins (9:11–14).

Crucial to the argumentation in these chapters is the author's adoption of a philosophical perspective akin to that of Platonism as a means through which to interpret Jewish institutions of worship. Plato taught that tangible, earthly objects were unreal. They were only reflections of their heavenly "forms," which incorporated their true essences. So for the author of Hebrews, Christ is the ultimate, true high priest of the heavenly sanctuary and tabernacle; those under Moses were only copies and shadows (8:1–6). The law as well was a shadow of the "true form of these realities" that was to come under Christ (10:1). In this way, the author reverses chronological priority, arguing that Christianity was not the successor of Israel and the Hebrew Bible but their heavenly antecedent, the genuine reality after which they were patterned.

Section three of Hebrews continues and buttresses the exhortation to faith and perseverance at the end of chapter 10 (vv. 35–39). In a sense, the author returns to the topic of the word of God, citing examples of faith from the characters and stories of the Hebrew Bible. These are the "great cloud of witnesses" (12:1) who surround the audience of the book of Hebrews and inspire them faithfully to endure persecution. This list of examples lays the foundation for the final exhortations of the book in its last two chapters.

Covenant in the Central Section

The word "covenant" (*diathēkē*) occurs seventeen times in the book of Hebrews (7:22; 8:6, 8, 9 [twice], 10; 9:4 [twice], 15 [twice], 16, 17, 20; 10:16, 29; 12:24; 13:20). All but two of these occurrences are in the central section, and only one of the remaining fifteen falls outside chapters 8—10. In 7:22, Jesus is called the "guarantor of a better covenant." He is the one who assures the availability of this covenant. The writer does not here explain exactly what this covenant is or why it is better. Rather, this verse sets the stage for the discussion in chapters 8—10, where covenant becomes the focal point.

Chapters 8—10 are the heart of the book of Hebrews and the climax of its christological argument. The content of these chapters may once have been an independent homily[7]: 8:1–6 introduces the basic theme of the contrast between heavenly and earthly sanctuaries that runs throughout this section; 8:8–12 quotes Jeremiah 31:31–34, and an exposition follows in 9:1—10:10; the rhetorical flourish in 10:11–18 summarizes the basic affirmation of the sermon and recalls the quotation from Jeremiah. But the section is now linked with what precedes. Hebrews 8:1 opens with the statement that the writer is now ready to present the main point. The Greek word translated "main point" by the NRSV (*kephalaion*) refers not to a summary of what precedes but to the conclusion to which it has led.[8] In other words, the discussion heretofore has been preliminary; this is the essence of the message of Hebrews. That message is that the system of priest-hood and sacrifice in the Hebrew Bible was but a shadow of the better, heavenly one that has now been revealed. In this better system, Jesus is the high priest who has "obtained a more excellent ministry" because he is the "mediator of a new covenant" (8:6). The high priest served as a representative of the people to God in the old system. Jesus is superior because he actually mediates a covenant between God and humanity.

In 8:7 the author launches the discussion of the contrast between the "old" and "new" covenants. The citation of Jeremiah 31:31–34 in Hebrews 8:8–12 is the longest quotation of a passage from the Hebrew Bible in the New Testament. It is partially quoted again in 10:16–17, marking the extent of the author's exposition. These two quotations account for five of the mentions of covenant in Hebrews (8:8, 9 [twice], 10; 10:16). The word *covenant* does not actually occur in the Greek text of 8:7, but that is clearly the antecedent of the word *first*. The first covenant was imperfect, thus necessitating a second one. Jeremiah's message of hope is interpreted by the author of Hebrews as a word of reproach. The "old" covenant was faulty because the people of Israel broke it so that a "new" one was required. The contrast between the two covenants is much sharper than that of other New Testament writers: "In speaking of 'a new covenant,' he has made the first one obsolete. And what is obsolete and growing old will soon disappear" (8:13, NRSV). Again, the word *covenant* does not actually appear in the Greek text here, but there is no doubt that it is what the author is referring to with the word "new (one)."

---

[7]Cf. Attridge, "Hebrews," *ABD* 2: 98. The following outline of this section is his.
[8]Lindars, *Theology of the Letter of Hebrews*, 79, n. 79.

This verse seems on the surface to go against the other New Testament passages in their reference to the "new" covenant as a refurbishing or renewal of previous covenants. But a closer look at Hebrews indicates that the contrast is not as strong as it first appears. The author of Hebrews is quoting Jeremiah 31, which, as we saw, locates the newness of the new covenant in its spiritual nature, as being inscribed on the heart. Hence, in chapters 9—10 Hebrews goes on to explain that what is obsolete about the first covenant is its ritual activities, specifically sacrifices, precisely because these cannot perfect or purify the conscience of the worshiper (9:9, 14), as could the once-for-all sacrifice of Christ.[9] In 9:15–17 the author also plays on the dual meaning of the Greek word *diathēkē* by saying that a will or testament (*diathēkē*) requires a death in order to go into effect. So the new covenant (*diathēkē*) is enacted by Christ's death. This contrast between the "new," spiritual or internal, covenant and the former exterior covenant is in agreement with the understanding expressed by Paul and the synoptic gospel writers. Indeed, the quotation in 9:20, "This is the blood of the covenant that God has ordained for you" (NRSV), alludes to and reinterprets Exodus 24:8, just as do Jesus' words at the Last Supper.

In 9:23 the author of Hebrews continues the image of Christ as high priest. The specific occasion is the day of atonement (*yôm kippūr*), and this is the only place in the New Testament where it is mentioned in connection with Jesus' death. Yom Kippur is the holiest day of the year in the Jewish calendar, when individuals acknowledge their sins and seek forgiveness. In ancient Israel it was the one day of the year when a human being—the high priest—was allowed to enter the innermost sanctuary of the temple—the "holy of holies" or "most holy place" in order to atone for the sins of the people by sprinkling sacrificial blood before the ark (Lev. 16). The high priest, however, had first to atone for his own sins. This system under the old covenant, therefore, was imperfect because the high priest was imperfect. Hence, the ritual of atonement had to be repeated every year. Moreover, the author of Hebrews says, animal blood cannot really take away sins. The new covenant is superior because its high priest is Christ, who is perfect and whose blood is truly effective in atoning for sins, so that his sacrifice is once for all time (Heb. 9:23—10:18).

---

[9]For further, more detailed discussion of this dimension of Hebrews see Susanne Lehne, *The New Covenant in Hebrews* (JSNTSup 44; Sheffield: JSOT Press, 1990).

It must be borne in mind, as Raymond Brown observes, that in all of this, the author of Hebrews does not intend for his readers to regard Christianity as a completely new religion; "it is an essential realization of the Old Testament promise."[10] Brown goes on to observe that in referring to the old covenant's being ineffective and even obsolete, the author of Hebrews does not mean that God's moral law has been abolished. Indeed, the author's point is that the old covenant was an imperfect version of the heavenly prototype. This is, admittedly, a kind supersessionism. But it is only the ceremonial laws of the Hebrew Bible that have been superseded. The moral laws, and in fact God's will for humanity, have hardly been superseded, because in the view of the author of Hebrews it is the foundation and essence of the covenant under Moses as well as the one under Jesus. Indeed, to an extent, they are one and the same.

The "Hall of Faith" (Chapter 11)

Covenant in the Bible, as we have seen, is a two-sided arrangement: divine commitment and human obligation. However, we have also seen several covenants that are promissory in nature and therefore seem to represent only one side of the bargain—God's commitment. Where is the human obligation in these covenants? Hebrews 11 answers this question. If the inscription of the law on people's hearts and minds and the forgiveness of their sins is God's side of the "new covenant," as expounded in chapters 8—10, the human side is faith.[11]

The heroes of faith in Hebrews 11 are all taken from the Hebrew Bible: Abel, Enoch, Noah, Abraham, Sarah, Isaac, Jacob, Joseph, Moses, Rahab, Gideon, Barak, Samson, Jephthah, David, and Samuel. This is another indication that the "new" covenant is simply a renewal of the "old" covenants. The response God calls for from his covenant partner is the same in all cases; it is faith. By repeating the phrase "by faith," the author distinguishes each of these individuals.

---

[10]Raymond Brown, *Christ Above All: The Message of Hebrews* (Downers Grove, Ill.: Intervarsity, 1982), 148.

[11]This observation about the two-sided covenant in Hebrews is Lindars' (*Theology of the Letter to the Hebrews,* 100).

In each of them the author finds a different characteristic of faith.[12] Faith is:

- the conviction of unseen realities (11:1)
- the recognition of God's power over creation (11:3)
- the understanding of how to please God like Abel, Enoch, and Noah (11:4–7)
- manifested in concrete acts of obedience like those of Abraham and Sarah (11:8–12, 17–19)
- trusting in God's promises and plan for the future like Jacob and Joseph (11:20–22)
- courageous in defiance of evil like Moses' parents (11:23)
- willing to endure suffering for justice and righteousness in the here and now in order to attain future rewards like Moses (11:24–28)
- open to God's working in unexpected ways like the Israelites at the Red Sea and Jericho and like Rahab (11:29–31)
- constant in devotion to God in victory but also in persecution (11:32–38)

The specific concern of the author of Hebrews is to encourage his readers to remain steadfast in their Christian faith in the face of the sufferings they are currently undergoing. But its enduring message for covenant lies in its call for loyalty and trust from the people of God to his magnanimous promises and blessings. This kind of faith is not simply an attitude or an intellectual assent to a series of propositions, but is a lifestyle encompassing concrete actions.

Covenant and Supersessionism

The careful consideration of the meaning of covenant in the New Testament passages provides an important counter against the problem of supersessionism. When the New Testament is read carefully, especially with the Hebrew Bible as its background, it becomes clear that the "new covenant" of Christianity stands squarely in the heritage of ancient Israel and its series of covenants with God. Indeed, the earliest Christians were all Jews, and their "new" religion was regarded as a sect of Judaism. Our treatment of the New Testament passages

---

[12]Compare the characteristics discerned from this passage by Brown, *Christ Above All,* 197–225; and Pfitzner, *Hebrews,* 170–71.

about covenant has shown that it is impossible to understand these passages, and indeed the New Testament as a whole, apart from its background in the Hebrew Bible. Nowhere is this clearer than in the book of Hebrews, which, as we have just seen, quotes extensively from the Hebrew Bible and makes frequent reference to its system of ritual sacrifice.

It is through the series of covenants in the Hebrew Bible especially that we learn of God's desire to establish a relationship with humans and see the history of the *divine commitment* to humans that supplies one side of the covenantal relationships. At the same time, in the Hebrew Bible we come to understand better what God wants of humans—the *human obligation* that God imposes on covenantal partners. While Christians no longer follow the ritual practices prescribed in the Hebrew Bible (such as sacrifice), they do value the same virtues and internal qualities that the Hebrew Bible lauds: faithfulness, obedience, loyalty, and love, to name a few. Many of these are ideals associated with covenant. In the chapter that follows we will explore some of the other ethical teachings and features of religion that these two great covenantal partners with God value.

The book of Hebrews, as we have just seen, refers to the practice of sacrifice prescribed in the first or "old" covenant (Sinai) as obsolete. At about the time Hebrews was written, Judaism was forced to abandon animal sacrifice. Worship in the temple was replaced by worship in synagogues; prayer took the place of sacrifice. As a result, today the practice of animal sacrifice does not divide Jews and Christians, because Jews no longer practice it. Hence, as we have seen, the designation "obsolete," as Hebrews 8:13 uses it, is not appropriate for Judaism. Christians in fact share with Jews such needs and activities as prayer, personal devotion, and community worship. Moreover, this example suggests that Christians could learn much from Judaism when it comes to the interpretation and application of scripture.

The main reason for the changes in Judaism at the time of the New Testament was the destruction of the temple in 70 C.E. The way in which Jews were able to adapt religiously to changes in historical and social circumstances holds lessons for contemporary Christians who seek to apply the Bible's message to a society and a worldview that are very different from those at the time when the Bible was written. In addition, the survival of Judaism in the wake of horrendous persecution over the centuries also offers lessons about faith and perseverance for modern Christians.

Supersessionism, then, is unwarranted and is not endorsed by the New Testament. Judaism is not defunct. Christians share many dimensions of their faith with Jews. They have a common scripture in the Hebrew Bible that is rich with instruction about God's interactions with human beings. They share a heritage in the history of covenants. They also agree about a faithful person's principal obligation toward God and toward one's fellow human beings. The topic of covenant, therefore, is rich with possibilities for fostering Jewish-Christian dialogue.

9

THE THEOLOGICAL NEXUS OF COVENANT

W e ended the last chapter with a glance at the *Shema'*. It is no accident that this essential confession of Judaism comes from Deuteronomy. In chapter 2, I suggested that the Deuteronomistic History had an enormous impact on the composition and theology of the Bible. The finding of the book of the law under Josiah (2 Kgs. 22), which was some form of what we know as Deuteronomy, gave rise to the composition of the Deuteronomistic History. Other writings followed applying the Deuteronomistic theology to new circumstances (Prophets), modifying it (Chronicles), or even challenging it (Job). Just as Deuteronomy was the springboard that gave rise to much of the rest of the Hebrew Bible, it is also the center from which the Bible's theology emanates. "[T]he fundamental questions of Old Testament theology are concentrated in a nutshell in Deuteronomy, and a proper theology of the Old Testament really has to have its center there."[1]

We have already caught glimpses of Deuteronomy's influence on the idea of covenant as it occurs in different parts of the Bible. Covenant is just one of a complex of themes presented as a package in Deuteronomy. Deuteronomy was the first actual theology of the Bible, because it was the first work to arrange various ideas into a single system of beliefs. It was Deuteronomy that first systematically promulgated the idea that Yahweh was one God and that Israel was the chosen people, delivered from bondage and living on land that was God's gift. It therefore came close to being a doctrine of monotheism and did formulate doctrines of salvation and election. Deuteronomy also anticipated the notion of God as spirit, present with his people but not physically so, in some sense transcendent and thus not limited by his presence on Earth. It is to Deuteronomy that Jews and Christians owe their identity as "people of the book," constitutionally bound to God and to each other by a set of rules they are to follow. Chief among these is the command to worship Yahweh exclusively. But there are also rules about social and ethical behavior and warnings about the consequences of disobedience. A glance at this set of ideas makes clear that the Bible, Judaism, Christianity, and indeed Western civilization would not exist as we know them without the book of Deuteronomy.

This complex of themes that revolves around covenant accounts for the different format of this chapter. The following surveys of themes related to covenant will each begin with Deuteronomy and then move to consider the relevance for modern, especially Christian, readers. This chapter differs from what precedes it in that it is substantially longer than previous chapters and actually represents the second part of the book. However, it seems appropriate to treat these themes as a single chapter in order to reinforce the idea that they are interrelated and all part of a nexus interwoven with the Bible's presentation of a covenant with God.

---

[1]Siegfried Herrmann, "Die konstructive Restauration: Das Deuteronomium als Mitte biblischer Theologie," in H. W. Wolff, ed., *Probleme biblischer Theologie: Gerhard von Rad zum 70. Geburtstag* (Munich: Chr. Kaiser, 1971), 156. The German reads: "… im Deuteronomium (Dtn) die Grundfragen alttestamentlicher Theologie in nuce konzentriert sind, und wahrhaftig eine Theologie des Alten Testaments dort ihr Zentrum zu haben hat, wenn sie sachgemäß sein soll."

God

The view of God in Deuteronomy was nothing short of revolutionary for ancient Israel, and it shaped the basic understanding of God that Jews and Christians (and Muslims) share to this day.

> We must regard this Deuteronomic development of the doctrine of God as the fullest and most significant of all the theological turning-points in the concept of deity which the Old Testament brings to our attention. At one stroke it combines ideas of divine transcendence, incorporeality, invisibility and universal sovereignty, and so breaks dramatically with the religious traditions which preceded it...God is made to appear altogether more distinct, more other-worldly and more personal in nature than in the older literature of the Old Testament.[2]

The Uniqueness of God

For the beginning of Deuteronomy's understanding of God we turn again to the *Shemaʻ* in Deuteronomy 6:4: "Hear O Israel, Yahweh our God, Yahweh is one." This statement has two meanings.[3] The first and most obvious is that Yahweh is to be the only God for Israel: "Yahweh is our one and only."[4] Deuteronomy represents the beginning of monotheism in Israel, although strictly speaking, the book itself is not monotheistic, since it does not claim that Yahweh is the only god.[5] The Decalogue (Ten Commandments), for instance, does not deny the existence of other gods or command belief in only one God but rather states, "You shall have no other gods *before* [or 'beside'] me" (Deut. 5:7; cf. also 32:7–8). It is in this sense that Yahweh is referred to as a "jealous God" (Deut. 4:24; 5:9; 6:15), because he does not permit allegiance to other deities. What Deuteronomy thus mandates is *practical* monotheism. The *Shemaʻ* makes clear that Yahweh is unique. There is no other god like Yahweh, who is the only God Israel is to worship, and who is not to be worshiped as part of a

---

[2]Clements, *Deuteronomy,* 53.

[3]On the different possible ways of translating this sentence see Albertz, *A History of Israelite Religion,* 206, n. 65.

[4]Georg Braulik, "Deuteronomy and the Birth of Monotheism," in *The Theology of Deuteronomy: Collected Essays of Georg Braulik, O.S.B.* (Dallas: BIBAL, 1994), 101.

[5]Ibid., esp. 100.

pantheon. For all practical purposes where Israel is concerned, Yahweh is the only God. Thus, Deuteronomy 7:9 can state unequivocally, "Yahweh your God is God." In Hebrew, the word God even has the article: "Yahweh your God is *the* God." The statement that Yahweh is *your* God still leaves the door open for the existence of other gods; they are not explicitly denied. But "we are on the threshold of monotheism."[6] Later additions to the book of Deuteronomy cross that threshold. This is especially true of 4:1–40, which explicitly states that "Yahweh is God; there is no other besides him" (v. 35). Since this chapter stands near the beginning of Deuteronomy, it furnishes a lens through which the entire book is read. It is not surprising, therefore, that the *Shema'*, although not originally fully monotheistic, came to represent the distinctive monotheism of Judaism and Christianity (and Islam)—its confession in, and call to, that belief.

The second meaning of the *Shema'* relates to the doctrine of *centralization*, which is one of Deuteronomy's key concepts. Centralization meant that the government, society, and religion of Israel (in reality Judah in the seventh century) were to be centered in Jerusalem. The idea was at least partly political and related to King Josiah's efforts to unite Judah politically, militarily, and economically in resistance against the Assyrian empire. But there was much more to centralization in Deuteronomy than this. In the ancient Near East, gods were regarded as appearing in different manifestations at different places. This meant that the same god could be worshiped and considered present at various shrines at the same time. As part of its centralization motif, Deuteronomy denies that this is the case with Yahweh. The *Shema'* says, in effect, that there are not separate manifestations of Yahweh at different sanctuaries; Yahweh is one and has only the single sanctuary in the Jerusalem temple.

This new view of God was not purely theoretical; centralization carried practical consequences.[7] The people are commanded to destroy all the cultic installations to other gods (12:2–4) in order to worship Yahweh exclusively. But even the worship of Yahweh is not to take place everywhere; it is to be limited to "the place that Yahweh your God will choose" (12:13–14), that is, Jerusalem. In the ancient

---

[6]Ibid., 113.

[7]See Bernard M. Levinson, *Deuteronomy and the Hermeneutics of Legal Innovation* (New York: Oxford University Press, 1997).

world slaughter of animals and eating of meat were typically done in connection with sacrifice. This practice is reflected in several stories in the Bible (esp. 1 Sam. 9:11–24; 14:32–35) and in the law in Leviticus 17:1–9, which explicitly forbids secular slaughter. As part of the same practice, priests were sustained by the allocation of a portion of the sacrifice (Deut. 18:1–5; cf. Lev. 6:16–18, 26–30; 7:6–10, 31–36; 1 Sam. 2:12–17). Deuteronomy's demand for centralization necessitated a change in this practice, because it was impossible for people to travel to Jerusalem each time they had to slaughter an animal for meat. Deuteronomy, therefore, made a distinction between ritual and secular slaughter. While sacrifices could only be offered at the temple in Jerusalem (Deut. 12:1–14), slaughtering an animal for meat was permitted anywhere (12:15–18). This meant further that the Levites who had officiated as priests at the local shrines outside Jerusalem were now out of a job and would have to be provided for by public assistance (12:19) or else move to Jerusalem to serve in the temple there (18:6–8). Deuteronomy's doctrine of "one Yahweh," then, called for a complete restructuring of life and society.

In short, the *Shema'* and the law of centralization in Deuteronomy demanded that there be one capital with one place of worship of one God by one people. This law easily lent itself to the doctrine of the exclusivity of the worship of Yahweh and then to monotheism. It would also be instrumental in the development of other important theological tenets, such as that of the election of the chosen people, which we shall explore below.

The Nature of God

Restricting the worship of Yahweh to one central sanctuary created a theological dilemma. It might leave the impression that God himself was somehow limited to that one location. The author(s) of Deuteronomy sought to overcome this problem by means of what has come to be called the "name theology."[8] Deuteronomy refers to Jerusalem as "the place where Yahweh will put his name" or "cause his name to dwell" (Deut. 12:5, 11). Yahweh's name in the Jerusalem temple represents him without making the claim that he is actually

---

[8]See Gerhard von Rad, *Studies in Deuteronomy,* 37–44; S. Dean McBride, "The Deuteronomic Name Theology," Ph.D. dissertation, Harvard University, 1969; Tryggve N. D. Mettinger, *The Dethronement of Sabaoth: Studies in the Shem and Kabod Theologies* (ConBOT 18; Lund: Gleerup, 1982), 38–79.

present there or limited to its precincts. God's actual dwelling, as Solomon expresses it in 1 Kings 8:27, is in heaven: "Will God indeed live on the earth? Heaven, even the highest heaven, cannot contain you, much less this temple that I have built." In this way the name theology preserved God's immanence, while at the same time it asserted his transcendence.[9]

The implications of this name theology for the understanding of the nature of God were enormous. First of all, if God could not be contained by heaven and could be both immanent and transcendent, then God had to be a spiritual entity rather than a corporeal one. For Deuteronomy especially this meant that the Divine could not be depicted in tangible objects; to attempt to do so was to diminish and insult God (Deut. 4:1–40).[10] Hence, images of any kind were strictly forbidden (Deut. 5:8–10). This included images that were meant to depict Yahweh; how much more for those portraying other gods. In this light, the harshness of the measures prescribed in Deuteronomy against idolatry and its practitioners can begin to be understood. The oneness and uniqueness of Yahweh called for purity of worship, which centralization was intended to ensure (German: *Kultuseinheit=Kultusreinheit*). Even the ark of the covenant, which is described elsewhere as Yahweh's throne and the representation of his presence in war (Num. 10:35–36; 1 Sam. 4:5–11; 2 Sam. 6:2; 2 Kgs. 19:14–15; Pss. 80:1; 99:1), in Deuteronomy becomes merely a chest in which the tablets and book of the law are deposited (Deut. 10:1–5; 31:25–26).

God's immanence—the presence of the "name" in the temple—is due to God's desire to build relationships with human beings. It is the deity who initiates relationships—such as covenants—between God and humans. God makes commitments to humans and keeps them. God is intimately concerned with and involved in human affairs. God, as spirit, is particularly interested in what goes on in the

---

[9]William M. Schniedewind (*Society and the Promise to David: The Reception History of 2 Samuel 7:1–17* [New York/Oxford: Oxford University Press, 1999], 96–97) has recently argued that the language of the name theology was borrowed from Assyrian royal inscriptions in which a king laid exclusive claim to a particular locale. Originally, therefore, the name theology in Deuteronomy was intended to affirm Yahweh's exclusive presence in the temple and not as an abstraction of his presence there. Schniedewind may be correct, but he also acknowledges that the abstraction of the name was a later Deuteronomistic development, and that is our concern here.

[10]Deuteronomy 4:1–40, which expounds on this matter at length, is widely regarded as an addition to the book. But the polemic against idols that it elaborates was already in the original book.

human heart or mind. Without denying the importance of ritual activities, Deuteronomy emphasizes the interior thoughts and attitude of the "heart," which Yahweh was able to perceive (Deut. 5:21; 7:17; 8:11–20; 9:4–5; 10:12–13; 11:13, 18; 15:7, 10; 26:16). Later authors within Deuteronomy's sphere of influence attached even more importance to the heart. Hence, the "new covenant" in Jeremiah 31, as we have seen, was to be completely a matter of the heart.

This view of God was largely responsible for the survival of Jewish faith in the exile and beyond. As mentioned in the last chapter, the temple, where Yahweh had caused Yahweh's name to dwell, was destroyed in 586 B.C.E., in effect bringing a halt to sacrifice and the other rituals carried on there. But because God was spirit and omnipresent, sacrifice was readily replaced by prayer as the means of contacting and placating the deity. The prayer of Solomon in 1 Kings 8 already represents an important step in this direction as it repeatedly asks that God, in heaven, hear the requests of his people, wherever they are, when they pray to him in the direction of the temple. Jesus takes this idea one step further in his conversation with the Samaritan woman in John 4:24: "God is spirit and those who worship him must worship in spirit and in truth." For Christians and for most modern Jews, worship and prayer need not be restricted to any single place but are a matter of the proper attitude of devotion toward the divine spirit.

Election

Centralization implies election. It is not just the place for Yahweh's name that Yahweh has chosen but Israel as his people (7:6–8; 10:14–15; 14:2). The concept of election was new with Deuteronomy. The idea that Yahweh was Israel's God was much older. But it was Deuteronomy that first expressed the notion that Yahweh had chosen Israel. It was Yahweh who initiated the covenant with Israel at the sacred mountain of Horeb when Yahweh brought them out of Egypt (5:2) and through the wilderness (8:14–16). Yahweh will now defeat the inhabitants of Canaan and deliver the land to Israel if they will but trust Yahweh and obey the law (7:16–26; 9:1–12; 11:22–25). The covenant is the tangible sign of Israel's election as a people and of the reliability of God's promises.

Like the name theology, the concept of the election of Israel presented a theological dilemma. As we have seen, for the authors of Deuteronomy, Yahweh was the only God. Other gods, if they existed at all, were to be ignored. Yahweh was the supreme God, sovereign over all gods, "*the* God of gods and Lord of lords" (10:17). Yahweh is Lord over all nations, and all creation: "To Yahweh your God belong the heaven and the highest heaven, the earth and all that is in it" (10:14). Yet, as both of these verses point out, Yahweh is Israel's unique God, the only God for Israel. But if Yahweh was Lord over all creation—all nations and peoples—then his special relationship with Israel might appear diluted. Not so, declares Deuteronomy. The concept of election allowed one to affirm Yahweh's supremacy while also retaining the uniqueness of his relationship with Israel. As Deuteronomy 10:15 goes on to explain, the supreme God, Yahweh, had chosen Israel as his privileged people. At the same time, it was the supremacy of Yahweh, and of later monotheism, that gave the doctrine of election its real force. It was one thing to be the people chosen by or assigned to one particular god among many. It was quite another to be the elect of the supreme God or the one and only God.

The original covenant was made at Horeb with the people who came out of Egypt.[11] Deuteronomy describes the renewal of the covenant with the generation that is about to enter the land (11:26–32; 27:1–14). Thus, the generation Moses is addressing in Deuteronomy was not alive at the time of the original covenant. Yet he tells them that the covenant is with them (5:3), and this later generation identifies with its ancestors who were slaves in Egypt (5:15; 6:21–23). As pointed out earlier, this idea of the inheritance of the covenant is what makes it still valid for later generations at the time of Josiah, when Deuteronomy was first written, and in the exile, when it was revised and incorporated into the Deuteronomistic History. In 2 Kings 23:1–3, the covenant into which the people enter is actually a renewal of the covenant in Deuteronomy, which is itself a renewal of the original covenant at Horeb. Those of every generation who have a covenant with God are the elect. Thus, teaching the commandments to children (Deut. 6:7) ensures the continuation of the covenant relationship with Yahweh for each generation.

The impact of this idea of election can scarcely be measured. It began the process of forging Jewish identity, not so much in national terms but in ethnic, and especially religious, terms. While Israel's

---

[11]The extension of the covenant back to Abraham is the result of later editing, as shown by Thomas Römer, *Israels Väter*. See also Römer, "The Book of Deuteronomy," in McKenzie and Graham, eds., *The History of Israel's Traditions,* esp. 205–8.

existence as a nation was near its end when Deuteronomy was written, Judaism was just beginning. The "chosen people" was not the nation of Israel but Jews, both ethnically and religiously. Deuteronomy established the uniqueness and separateness of this people who professed only one God. Later on, Christians would emphasize the religious element of election and argue that being God's chosen was not a matter of ethnicity but of faith. For both Jews and Christians, the belief that they are God's chosen people is crucial, because it is such people who are the prime targets of God's love. The doctrine of election, which began in Deuteronomy, therefore, remains to this day an important ingredient of both Judaism and Christianity.

Deuteronomy uses a special term, *sᵉgûllāh* (meaning "special property," Deut. 7:6; 14:2; 26:18; cf. Exod. 19:5; Ps. 135:4), to describe Israel's privileged status before God among the nations.[12] The people of Israel are Yahweh's "special property" because he has a covenantal relationship with them. This is the point of Amos 3:2: "You only have I known of all the families of the earth" (NRSV). The verb "to know" in Hebrew can be used for an intimate relationship between people—including, but not limited to, a sexual relationship. Amos says that Yahweh has a relationship only with Israel among the nations; they are his *sᵉgûllāh*. But if being the "special property" of the supreme God should tend to make the people so designated arrogant and self-satisfied in their election, another look at Deuteronomy undermines this tendency. The choosing of Israel, it says, was not based on any traits inherent in Israel itself. It was not because of Israel's size among the nations (Deut. 7:7–8) or because Israel was more righteous or otherwise deserving (9:5). It was rather because of Yahweh's love for them (7:7). What is more, with election comes responsibility. The passage from Amos 3:2 quoted earlier ("You only have I known of all the families of the earth") continues, "therefore I will visit all your iniquities upon you." As Yahweh's chosen, who were privy to the divine will, Amos says the people of Israel will be judged especially closely for their misbehavior. Later, in Amos 9, the prophet says that just as Yahweh brought Israel from Egypt, he controlled the movements of other peoples, such as the Philistines and Arameans (v. 7). The threat is implicit: While Israel alone has a covenant with Yahweh, they can be replaced by the God who is over all nations. Verse 8 is

---

[12]Weinfeld, *Deuteronomy,* 62, 368.

more explicit as Yahweh threatens to destroy the "sinful kingdom" from the face of the earth.

Jews and Christians are God's chosen covenant people, his "special property." But they have no reason to gloat, because their election is based not on merit, but on divine love. It also invests them with special responsibility to live in such a way as to exemplify God's love and will for all people.

Community

In articulating the doctrine of election, Deuteronomy expressed the concept of Israel as a single people for the first time. The idea that Yahweh chose Israel at the exodus because of his love for them is found in earlier prophetic literature (Hos. 11:1). But Deuteronomy expanded the idea outside the confines of family relationships and extended it to an entire nation and ethnic group. The framework of the book describes "all Israel" (1:1) gathered to hear Moses on the plain of Moab and to renew the covenant with Yahweh. The core of the book and the laws themselves are addressed to Israel as a whole, united people and nation (5:1; 6:4; 9:1; etc.). This portrait of a unified Israel is due in part to the historical circumstances in which Deuteronomy was written. A century earlier, the former Northern Kingdom of Israel had been decimated by the Assyrians, many of its people carried into exile, and their land resettled as Assyrian provinces by captives from elsewhere. Some of the Israelites who escaped fled to Judah, which helps to account for the relationship of Deuteronomy with Hosea and perhaps other northern traditions. Josiah apparently even tried to control matters in the north (2 Kgs. 23:15–20) and perhaps saw himself as king of Israel as well as Judah. Deuteronomy sought to incorporate the traditions of the north and to appeal to its remnant to join in Josiah's reform. It thus reflected an attempt at consolidation in opposition to the Assyrian threat. But whatever its origin, the idea of a united Israel was a turning point in self-identity of the "children of Israel."

The election of Israel as a nation or people rather than as individuals bears an important lesson about the "horizontal" dimension of faith. The lesson is pertinent more for Christians than for Jews, who have a much better sense in general of the value of the faith community. Christians sometimes speak of election as the establishment of a personal relationship with God or Christ and thereby neglect the role of the community. In addition to the example of

Deuteronomy, they would do well to consider the little book of 1 John in the New Testament.[13] It addresses the value of community, urging its audience to *remain* (a key word in the book) in the fellowship of other Christians. For instance, 1 John 1:7 locates the church community as the place where forgiveness takes place when it says, "If we walk in the light as he himself is in the light, we have fellowship with one another, and the blood of Jesus his Son cleanses us from all sin (NRSV)."

Reward and Punishment

What is riding on Israel's obedience to the covenant in Deuteronomy is nothing less than its status as God's chosen people and its survival in the promised land. The gift of the land is a particularly important theme in Deuteronomy 5—11 with the portrait of Israel poised to enter Canaan. The land is a good and bountiful land, "flowing with milk and honey" (6:3, 11; 7:13–14; 8:7–10; 11:9–14). Its current residents are powerful giants (9:1–3); but Yahweh promised the land to the ancestral Israelites (6:10, 18; 7:1; 8:1; 9:5; 10:11; 11:9, 21). The fact that their descendants now stand ready to enter the land attests to Yahweh's faithfulness to a promise. Yahweh brought them out of Egypt (6:12, 21–23; 7:8–9; 11:2–4) and then preserved them in the wilderness (8:2–4; 9:6–29; 11:5–7), all because of that promise. Israel, therefore, may rest assured that Yahweh is both powerful and faithful enough to complete the promise by bringing them into the land. Hence, the burden for acquiring and retaining the land falls upon the people and depends on their obedience (5:33; 11:26–32) and that of their children (6:2, 6–9, 20–25; 11:18–21) to the divine commands. Disobedience would result in the loss of the land and the expulsion of the people (8:19–20; 11:16–17). The ceremony on Mounts Ebal and Gerizim described near the end of Deuteronomy (27—28) lays out the alternatives: blessings for obedience, unspeakable curses for disobedience.

The contingency of Israel's tenure on the land in Deuteronomy is again closely related to the historical situation in which the book was written. As we have seen, a century before Josiah the Northern Kingdom of Israel was, in effect, destroyed by the Assyrians. This event must have been taken as verification of the threats of the eighth-century prophets, such as Hosea and Amos. The authors of

---

[13]See Steven L. McKenzie, "The Church in 1 John," *RQ* 19 (1976): 211–16.

Deuteronomy developed the prophetic message into a simple but far-reaching theological doctrine: Sin brings punishment, faithfulness reward. This doctrine fit perfectly within Deuteronomy's covenantal theology, which made use of the curses from Assyrian vassal treaties. Israel's loyalty was to be to Yahweh. Unfaithfulness in the form of disobedience to the law would bring on the curses. The later Deuteronomistic historian would find in this doctrine an explanation not only for the fall of Israel but also for that of Judah.

The impact of this aspect of Deuteronomy's doctrine on modern faith is apparent—it is one of the sources for the Christian belief in ultimate reward or punishment after this life in heaven or hell. Yet it is difficult to know what to do with this doctrine. Christians themselves struggle with the issue of ultimate punishment. Perhaps it is best simply to take Deuteronomy at face value and recognize that there are consequences for covenant breaking, whether we fully understand them or not. Perhaps also it is more important to stress the positive: There are rewards for covenantal faithfulness. Moreover, it is important not to lose sight of the fact that the ideal motivation for faithfulness in Deuteronomy is not the fear of punishment or hope of reward, but the response in kind to the gracious deeds of God.

Scripture

The book of the law purportedly found in the temple under Josiah and identified as an early form of Deuteronomy is called the "book of the covenant" (2 Kgs. 23:2). This book contained laws; indeed, the bulk of it is preserved in Deuteronomy 12—26, which is commonly referred to as the "law code." But it was more than a collection of laws, first, because it also contained other types of material, and second, because as a whole it was much more than the sum of its parts.

The term "law" is somewhat misleading, especially in an American context where there is a separation of church and state. Deuteronomy does contain legislation relating to civil matters—what constitutes various kinds of crimes and how they are to be punished. But to call it law is a misnomer for two reasons. First, because even the civil laws deal with religious matters—cultic celebrations and personnel, ritual cleanness, sacrifices, and the like. Even the rules for warfare concern "holy war" (Deut. 20). Second, the "law code" in chapters 12—26, and even more the introduction to it in chapters 1—11, are shot through and through with parenesis (preaching).

Often, this comes in the form of the rationale for specific laws. One is to treat the poor or disadvantaged in a certain way, remembering "that you were slaves in the land of Egypt" who were rescued by Yahweh (e.g., 24:17–22). Certain laws are designed to avoid "the abominable practices" of Israel's predecessors in Canaan (18:9). Rules about sexual relations are given in order to avoid "abomination" and bringing "guilt upon the land" that Yahweh is giving (e.g., 24:1–4). Even matters of personal hygiene (23:13–16) and finance (23:20–21) are grounded in religious considerations: "For Yahweh your God walks around within your camp…so your camp should be holy" (23:16) and "so that Yahweh your God may bless you" (23:21). While many of the laws in Deuteronomy are closely paralleled by those in other ancient Near Eastern codes, such as the Code of Hammurabi, the parenetic tone and focus on religious matters in Deuteronomy distinguish it as having something of a different nature from such codes.

Just as Deuteronomy is not really a treaty, so it is not really law either. It is address—preaching or teaching. Its laws, couched in parenetic form, are "instruction" or "teaching," which is what the Hebrew word *tôrāh,* usually translated "law," really means anyway. But as a document directed to Israel as a whole, Deuteronomy is something more than a collection of laws—even instructive ones. As we have seen, Deuteronomy presents an entire theological system. The "instruction" in Deuteronomy—both laws and parenesis—is a comprehensive program for the people of Israel; it is, in short, Israel's *constitution.* It is worth recalling that the book of Deuteronomy first expresses the concept of Israel as a whole people—God's chosen people. The "book of the law" represents the constitution for this people as a national, ethnic, and religious identity.

It is in the category of religion that Deuteronomy has exercised the most influence. The chosen people are bound together and to Yahweh by this single, distinctive book, "*the* book of the law," as the guide to their lives individually and in community. The idea of such a book—a unique, holy, authoritative book—containing the comprehensive divine law is the idea of scripture. Whether the original author of Deuteronomy saw the book in these terms is open to question, but it is clearly presented this way in 2 Kings 23, as well as in the finished form of Deuteronomy itself (Deut. 30:10; 31:26). "The term 'Book of the Law' (*sēfer hattôrāh*) as a sanctified authoritative work which contains all the divine law is encountered for the first time in

Israel's history in the account of the reform of Josiah (2 Kgs. 22—23)."[14] Of course, the content of scripture was not long limited to Deuteronomy. Other works were written for inclusion in that category. But the process began with Deuteronomy. It is somewhat ironic that the book that forbade adding to the divine command should spark such a process (4:2; 13:1). But that is what happened with Deuteronomy; it was the beginning of the Bible as Holy Scripture. The propagation of Deuteronomy's demand for adherence to its instruction led to Judaism and subsequently Christianity (and following the same principle even later, Islam) being "religions of the book."

Deuteronomy not only represents the beginning of scripture, but it also furnishes an important example for people of faith when it comes to the use and interpretation of scripture. According to Deuteronomy 5:1–21 (cf. 4:13), the original covenant on Mount Horeb contained not the entire law code in chapters 12—26, but only the Decalogue, or Ten Commandments. The more extensive law code in chapters 12—26 belongs to the form of the covenant being renewed with the later generation at the end of the wilderness wandering. Hence, the name "Deuteronomy," which means "second law." Deuteronomy places the second, longer code between the accounts of the ceremony on Mounts Ebal and Gerizim in chapters 11 and 27.

There are two versions of the Ten Commandments in the Bible—one in Deuteronomy 5 and the other in Exodus 20. The two vary only slightly, but some of their differences are significant. For example, Deuteronomy 5:12–15 commands the keeping of the Sabbath for reasons of social justice—so as to give a day of rest to all of the slaves and workers and other members (including animals) of a household. It concludes with the admonition, "You shall remember that you were a slave in the land of Egypt and Yahweh your God brought you out from there with a strong hand and an outstretched arm; therefore Yahweh your God commands you to observe the sabbath day." The P version (Exod. 20:8–11), on the other hand, grounds the Sabbath observance in its version of creation (Gen. 1:1—2:3), according to which God made the world in six days and rested on the seventh. These two versions may be read as different interpretations of the Ten Commandments for later settings, although that is probably not the way in which they originated.

---

[14]Cf. Weinfeld, "Deuteronomy," 174.

The Decalogue has long been the subject of intense scholarly attention.[15] Recent treatments indicate that it is not Mosaic, as was once thought, but originated with the book of Deuteronomy, perhaps even in its role as the introduction to the Deuteronomistic History.[16] In other words, the two versions of the Decalogue in Deuteronomy 5 and Exodus 20 probably do not both derive from a common prototype that each version modified in its own direction. Rather, the Exodus version is a revision of the one in Deuteronomy, as the following considerations suggest.

First, there is widespread assent that the version of the Decalogue in Exodus 20:1–17 is an insertion. It obviously interrupts the narrative about God's appearance on Mount Sinai and the people's fear in 19:16–25, which continues with 20:18. The people in 20:18–20 do not acknowledge receipt of the Ten Commandments and in fact ask that God not speak to them (v. 19), which strongly suggests that they have not just heard God's words in 20:1–17. The version in Deuteronomy 5:6–21, by contrast, is well suited to its context. The Decalogue in Deuteronomy is the substance of the law and covenant written on the stone tablets received at Horeb, which is then elaborated and renewed in the rest of the book with the people on the plains of Moab. Also, while the Decalogue in the form of a speech from God does not fit well with its surroundings in Exodus, its exhortative style is appropriate in the introduction to the law code in Deuteronomy. The lateness of the insertion in the Exodus version of the Decalogue and its Deuteronomic origin are indicated by the fact that the grounds for keeping the Sabbath in Exodus 20:8–11 are distinctly priestly in language and ideology (cf. Gen. 1:1—2:3), and P is widely considered later than Deuteronomy. Also, the reference to Yahweh speaking from heaven and the concern to establish his exclusiveness in Exodus 20:22–23 suggest that the author of these verses was familiar not only with the Deuteronomic Decalogue but also with its broader context in Deuteronomy 4—5, and that Deuteronomy 4:1–40 is a late addition to the book.

---

[15]For a history of scholarship up to about 1960 see J. J. Stamm, *The Ten Commandments in Recent Research* (SBT; Naperville, Ill.: Allenson, 1967). Cf. also Clements, *Deuteronomy,* 38–42. On more recent scholarship see the detailed treatment by Weinfeld, *Deuteronomy 1–11,* 236–327.

[16]See esp. Frank-Lothar Hossfeld, *Der Decalog: Seine späten Fassungen, die originale Komposition und seine Vorstufen* (OBO 45; Fribourg: Universitätsverlag, 1982); Mayes, *Deuteronomy,* 161–65; E. W. Nicholson, "The Decalogue as the Direct Address of God," *VT 27* (1977): 422–33.

The concern of the Decalogue for Israel's exclusive worship of Yahweh suggests its Deuteronomic origin. It surfaces especially clearly in the shared reference to Yahweh as a "jealous God" (Exod. 20:5// Deut. 5:9), which "can only be understood in the context of turning to the worship of other gods, not that of setting up an image of Yahweh." "While it is not impossible that such a concern existed in pre-deuteronomic times it is from this time that it gets its closest parallel in the commands for the single sanctuary and for the abolition of all non-Yahwistic shrines and forms of worship in Dt. 12f."[17] This origin is confirmed by the other examples of Deuteronomic language found in the Exodus version as well as in Deuteronomy: "the house of slaves," "carved image" and "likeness," "those who hate me" and "those who love me," "the resident alien in your gate," and "that your days may be prolonged."[18]

Two passages outside of Deuteronomy are often cited as presupposing the existence of the Decalogue. These are Hosea 4:2 ("There is swearing, lying, killing, stealing, and committing adultery") and Jeremiah 7:9 ("Will you steal, murder, commit adultery, swear falsely, burn incense to Baal, and go after other gods whom you do not know...?). But neither of these verses demonstrates the existence of the Decalogue as we have it in Exodus and Deuteronomy. It is not clear that either list presupposes any earlier document; they could simply be a general list of social offenses regarded by Hosea and Jeremiah as especially egregious. If an earlier list does underlie either verse, it does not follow the order or reflect the entirety of the Decalogue. Together, these two verses may be seen as confirming a late seventh-century date for the Decalogue, since they suggest that the content and order of Exodus 20 and Deuteronomy 5 had not become fixed by the time of Jeremiah's temple sermon at the beginning of Josiah's reign (Jer. 26:1). Individual prohibitions in the Decalogue certainly existed before that time, maybe even in smaller collections. But it was "the bringing together of these issues and the making of them into a matter of primary, and ultimate, commitment to Yahweh as God" that was Deuteronomy's innovation.[19]

---

[17]Mayes, *Deuteronomy,* 167 and 164, respectively.

[18]This list is taken from Weinfeld (*Deuteronomy 1–11,* 243), who refers to these as "phrases that look Deuteronomic" but argues, unconvincingly in my view, that they indicate the northern, not Deuteronomic, provenance of the Decalogue.

[19]Clements, *Deuteronomy,* 42.

While the Ten Commandments as a document shared by Exodus 20 and Deuteronomy 5 probably arose in connection with the Deuteronomic law book and the reform coordinated with it during the reign of Josiah, there are some hints that it was inserted into its present context in Deuteronomy 5 at an even later date by the Deuteronomistic Historian. For one thing, the parenetic introduction to the Deuteronomic law beginning at 6:4 neither presupposes nor mentions the Decalogue. In addition, the Decalogue uses the second personal singular, while the material around it is in the second plural.[20] In short, whether it was part of the original book of Deuteronomy or was inserted later by Dtr,

> As a general point we cannot fail to recognize the significance of the conclusion that the Ten Commandments, which have formed so important a legacy of the religious and social meaning of the Old Testament, are to be seen as a product of the Deuteronomic movement.[21]

As this quotation implies, the Ten Commandments have played a formative role in Judaism and Christianity. In a real sense, the rest of the *tôrāh* in Deuteronomy is an elaboration of the Decalogue, a longer "second" version of the original, fundamental law. When Jesus gave the "new law" in his Sermon on the Mount (Matt. 5—7), he expounded on the real meaning of at least some of the commandments in the Decalogue. Even today, the Ten Commandments continue to be seen as the basic statement of morality in the Western world. In many ways they form the basis of civil law in our own society. It is in the elaboration of the Decalogue that Deuteronomy furnishes a valuable lesson about the interpretation of scripture. The Ten Commandments are an element of covenantal theology, because they are the stipulations of the original covenant at Horeb. That covenant is reiterated with later generations. But it is not static. It must

---

[20]The mixture between singular and plural addressees (German: *Numeruswechsel*) is disputed as an indicator for separating later additions from the original Deuteronomy. But this seems to be a case in which it coincides with a change of writers. See Duane L. Christensen, *Deuteronomy 1–11* (WBC 6A; Dallas: Word, 1991), xlix–li, 33–34; Römer, "Book of Deuteronomy," 184–85; and Weinfeld, *Deuteronomy 1–11*, 15–16. Weinfeld (p. 16) characterizes the current consensus regarding the *Numeruswechsel*: "In sum, although in some cases the interchange of singular and plural address may indicate the existence of different layers, in general the interchange reflects stylistic variations introduced by the same author."

[21]Clements, *Deuteronomy*, 42.

be interpreted for each generation. Moses interprets it for the people about to enter Canaan; Jesus interprets it for his followers.

So it is with scripture—and there are two important stages in the process of interpretation. Like Jesus, the faithful must try to get at the real intent of the scripture's teachings. They must be careful not to confuse priorities. They must remember the principle that the law (and scripture) were made for humans, not humans for the law (Mark 2:23–28). Like Moses, they must consider the fact that changes in outlook from generation to generation call for differences in the way in which scripture is applied. Again, Christians would do well to look to Judaism, especially Conservative and Reform denominations, for the way in which it has learned to stress the spirit of the law and to be flexible where the letter is concerned. In this respect, Jesus and much of Judaism agree.

Covenantal Virtues

Obedience

We have subscribed to the characterization of covenant as "divine commitment and human obligation," so that it will come as no surprise to learn that Israel's primary virtue as a covenant partner is that of obeying the stipulations of the covenant in the form of the law that it incorporates. What may be surprising, though, is some of the language used to express this obligation of obedience. For instance, we have seen that the *Shema'* summarizes the principal duty of humans in both the Hebrew Bible and the New Testament as *loving* God with all of one's being. We observed in chapter 2 that "love" and "hate" are covenantal terminology, widely attested to in ancient Near Eastern treaties. Those who "love" the suzerain keep the stipulations of the covenant with him; those who "hate" him do not. This love for God, therefore, is not an emotional response, but obedience to the divine commands.

Another word for much this same virtue is *faithfulness*. It is this virtue whose absence is especially denounced in the passages in Hosea and Ezekiel that were treated in chapter 4. These passages use the analogy of marriage to depict the relationship between Yahweh and Israel. The prime stipulation of Deuteronomy's covenant to which this virtue relates is "You shall have no other gods before me" (Deut. 5:7). For Deuteronomy, keeping the covenant above all meant the exclusive worship of Yahweh.

The most remarkable word in this sphere of meaning is the Hebrew word *ḥesed*. It is a word that is difficult to translate because it incorporates a whole range of meanings.[22] In the NRSV it is often translated "steadfast love." But depending on the context in which it is used, it can also connote such things as faithfulness, kindness, love, loyalty, mercy, and truthfulness. It is perhaps misleading to call *ḥesed* a covenantal virtue, because it transcends the covenantal relationship. It may be thought of as the prime virtue in ancient Israel for any relationship. Thus, Ruth, in the book by her name, exhibits great *ḥesed* toward her mother-in-law, Naomi, even though there is, strictly speaking, no covenant between them. At the same time, *ḥesed* expresses the right attitude and behavior of the partners in a covenant.

The covenant between Yahweh and Israel is itself an act of *ḥesed* on Yahweh's part toward his people. Yahweh's keeping of his promises to Israel and to David, often in spite of their transgressions of the covenant, is also *ḥesed*. Yahweh's *ḥesed* calls for reciprocal behavior from Israel. They are to maintain *ḥesed* toward the covenant and toward God. In these terms, *ḥesed* might be thought of as "loving loyalty"—on the part of Yahweh toward the people to whom he has committed himself and on the part of Israel toward their God whose deeds and covenant have obligated them.

Social Justice

The second greatest commandment of the covenant is to love one's neighbor as oneself. In addition to the "vertical" obligation of Israelites to God, the covenant also charges them with a strong "horizontal" obligation toward each other. This involves justice for people of all social strata (16:18–20). But it also involves special consideration for the underprivileged—widows, orphans, and resident aliens (24:17–22). The reason, as we have already noted also in Deuteronomy's law of the Sabbath (5:12–15), is that the Israelites know what it is to be oppressed, so their treatment of one another should reflect the mercy they have received from God's hand.

---

[22]See the treatments of the term by Katherine Doob Sakenfeld, *The Meaning of Ḥesed in the Hebrew Bible: A New Inquiry* (HSM 17; Missoula, Mont.: Scholars Press, 1978); and Gordon R. Clark, *The Word Ḥesed in the Hebrew Bible* (JSOTSup 157; Sheffield: Sheffield Academic Press, 1993). See also the more recent and less technical treatments by Sakenfeld, *Faithfulness in Action: Loyalty in Biblical Perspective* (OBT; Philadelphia: Fortress Press, 1985); and "Love (OT)," *ABD* 4:375–81.

Once more, Deuteronomy offers a powerful message for people of faith in the modern era. Its stress on social justice, like its concern for the covenantal community, speaks strongly against the tendency of many modern Christians to see religion as purely a matter of an individual or personal relationship with God. What is more, Deuteronomy calls for pragmatic action on the part of faith communities in order to ensure social justice and mercy. This means providing the necessities of life for people who need them. It also means working for equitable treatment in the legal system for all persons regardless of race, ethnicity, and other such factors. Unfortunately, synagogues and churches have not always been on the right side in the struggles for civil rights and social justice. Only now are we beginning to grasp the instruction of the book of Deuteronomy.

BIBLIOGRAPHY

Albertz, Rainer. *A History of Israelite Religion in the Old Testament Period.* Vol. 1, *From the Beginnings to the End of the Monarchy.* OTL. Louisville, Ky.: Westminster/John Knox Press, 1994.

Anderson, Bernhard W. "Covenant." In Bruce M. Metzger and Michael D. Coogan, eds., *The Oxford Companion to the Bible,* 138–39. New York: Oxford University Press, 1993.

Attridge, Harold W. "Hebrews, Epistle to the." In David Noel Freedman, ed., *The Anchor Bible Dictionary,* 6 vols., 3:97–105, New York: Doubleday, 1992.

Auld, A. Graeme. "The Former Prophets: Joshua, Judges, 1–2 Samuel, 1–2 Kings." In Steven L. McKenzie and M. Patrick Graham, eds., *The Hebrew Bible Today: An Introduction to Critical Issues,* 53–68. Louisville, Ky.: Westminster John Knox Press, 1998.

Barr, James. "Some Semantic Notes on Covenant." In Herbert Donner, Robert Hanhart, and Rudolf Smend, eds., *Beiträge zur alttestamentlichen Theologie: Festschrift für Walther Zimmerli zum 70. Geburtstag,* 23–38. Göttingen: Vandenhoeck & Ruprecht, 1977.

Batey, Richard A. *The Letter of Paul to the Romans.* The Living Word Commentary. Austin, Tex.: Sweet, 1969.

Behm, Johannes. "διαθηκη." In Gerhard Kettel and Gerhard Friedrich, eds., Geoffrey W. Bromiley, trans., *Theological Dictionary of the New Testament,* 9 vols., 2:106–34. Grand Rapids, Mich.: Eerdmans, 1974.

Betz, Hans Dieter. "Corinthians, Second Epistle to the." In David Noel Freedman, ed., *The Anchor Bible Dictionary,* 6 vols., 1:1148–54. New York: Doubleday, 1992.

———. "Galatians." In David Noel Freedman, ed., *The Anchor Bible Dictionary,* 6 vols., 2:872–74. New York: Doubleday, 1992.

Botterweck, G. Johannes, and Helmer Ringgren, eds. *Theological Dictionary of the Old Testament.* 9 vols. Trans. John T. Willis and David Green. Grand Rapids, Mich.: Eerdmans, 1974–1998.

Braulik, Georg. *The Theology of Deuteronomy: Collected Essays of Georg Braulik, O.S.B.* Trans. U. Lindblad. Richland Hills, Tex.: BIBAL, 1994.

Brown, Francis, S. R. Driver, and Charles A. Briggs, *A Hebrew and English Lexicon of the Old Testament.* Oxford: Clarendon Press, 1974.

Brown, Raymond. *Christ Above All: The Message of Hebrews.* Downers Grove, Ill.: Intervarsity Press, 1982.

Carroll, Robert P. *Jeremiah: A Commentary.* OTL. Philadelphia: Westminster Press, 1986.

Christensen, Duane L. *Deuteronomy 1—11.* WBC 6A. Dallas: Word, 1991.

Clark, Gordon R. *The Word H̥esed in the Hebrew Bible.* JSOTSup 157. Sheffield: Sheffield Academic Press, 1993.

Clements, R. E. *Deuteronomy.* OTG. Sheffield: JSOT Press, 1989.

Clifford, Richard J. "Psalm 89: A Lament over the Davidic Ruler's Continued Failure." *HTR* 73 (1980): 35–47.

Crenshaw, James L. *Education in Ancient Israel: Across the Deadening Silence.* ABRL. New York: Doubleday, 1998.

Cross, Frank Moore. *Canaanite Myth and Hebrew Epic: Essays in the History of the Religion of Israel.* Cambridge/London: Harvard University Press, 1973.

———. *From Epic to Canon: History and Literature in Ancient Israel.* Baltimore/London: Johns Hopkins University Press, 1998.

Dentan, R. C. "The Literary Affinities of Exodus 34:6f." *VT* 13 (1963): 34–51.

Eichrodt, Walther. *Theology of the Old Testament.* OTL. Vol. 1. Trans. J. A. Baker. Philadelphia: Westminster Press, 1961.

———. *Theology of the Old Testament.* OTL. Vol. 2. Trans. J. A. Baker. Philadelphia: Westminster Press, 1967.

Fitzmyer, Joseph A. *The Aramaic Inscriptions of Sefire.* BibOr 19. Rome: Pontifical Biblical Institute, 1967.

——. *Romans.* AB 33. New York: Doubleday, 1993.

Freedman, David Noel. "Divine Commitment and Human Obligation: The Covenant Theme." *Interp* 18 (1964): 419–31.

——, ed. *The Anchor Bible Dictionary.* 6 vols. New York: Doubleday, 1992.

Friedman, Richard E. *The Exile and Biblical Narrative.* HSM 22. Chico, Calif.: Scholars Press, 1981.

——. "From Egypt to Egypt: Dtr1 and Dtr2." In Baruch Halpern and Jon D. Levenson, eds., *Traditions in Transformation,* 167–92. Winona Lake, Ind.: Eisenbrauns, 1981.

——. *Who Wrote the Bible?* Englewood Cliffs, N.J.: Prentice-Hall, 1987.

Furnish, Victor Paul. *II Corinthians.* AB 32A. Garden City, N.Y.: Doubleday, 1984.

——. "Ephesians, Epistle to the." In David Noel Freedman, ed., *The Anchor Bible Dictionary,* 6 vols., 2:535–42. New York: Doubleday, 1992.

Ha, John. *Genesis 15: A Theological Compendium of Pentateuchal History.* BZAW 181. Berlin/New York: Walter de Gruyter, 1989.

Halpern, Baruch. *The First Historians: The Hebrew Bible and History.* San Francisco: Harper & Row, 1988.

Hanson, Paul D. "The Song of Heshbon and David's *Nîr.*" *HTR* 61 (1968): 297–320.

Hayes, John H. "Covenant." In Watson E. Mills, et al., eds., *Mercer Dictionary of the Bible,* 177–81. Macon, Ga.: Mercer University Press, 1990.

Herrmann, Siegfried. "Die konstructive Restauration: Das Deuteronomium als Mitte biblischer Theologie." In H. W. Wolff, ed., *Probleme biblischer Theologie: Gerhard von Rad zum 70. Geburtstag,* 155–70. Munich: Chr. Kaiser, 1971.

Hess, Richard S. "The Slaughter of the Animals in Genesis 15." In Richard Hess, Gordon J. Wenham, and P. E. Satterthwaite, eds., *He Swore an Oath: Biblical Themes from Genesis 12–50,* 55–65. Grand Rapids, Mich.: Baker, 1992.

Hillers, Delbert R. *Treaty Curses and the Old Testament Prophets.* BibOr 16. Rome: Pontifical Biblical Institute, 1964.

————. *Covenant: The History of a Biblical Idea.* Seminars in the History of Ideas. Baltimore/London: Johns Hopkins Press, 1969.

Holladay, William L. *Jeremiah 2: A Commentary on the Book of the Prophet Jeremiah Chapters 26–52.* Hermeneia. Minneapolis: Fortress Press, 1989.

Hoppe, Leslie J. *The Origins of Deuteronomy.* Ph.D. dissertation. Northwestern University, 1978.

Hossfeld, Frank-Lothar. *Der Decalog: Seine späten Fassungen, die originale Komposition und seine Vorstufen.* OBO 45. Fribourg: Universitätsverlag, 1982.

Hughes, Philip Edgcumbe. "Hebrews, The Letter to the." In Bruce M. Metzger and Michael D. Coogan, eds., *The Oxford Companion to the Bible,* 274–77. New York: Oxford University Press, 1993.

Jenni, Ernst, and Claus Westermann, eds. *Theological Lexicon of the Old Testament.* Trans. Mark E. Biddle. Peabody, Mass.: Hendrickson, 1997.

Kettel, Gerhard, and Gerhard Friedrich, eds. *Theological Dictionary of the New Testament.* 9 vols. Trans. Geoffrey W. Bromiley. Grand Rapids, Mich.: Eerdmans, 1974.

Knoppers, Gary N. "Ancient Near Eastern Royal Grants and the Davidic Covenant: A Parallel?" *JAOS* 116 (1996): 670–97.

————. "David's Relation to Moses: The Contexts, Content and Conditions of the Davidic Promises." In John Day, ed., *King and Messiah in Israel and the Ancient Near East: Proceedings of the Oxford Old Testament Seminar,* 91–118. JSOTSup 270. Sheffield: Sheffield Academic Press, 1998.

Kreitzer, Larry. *2 Corinthians.* NTG. Sheffield: Sheffield Academic Press, 1996.

Kutsch, Ernst. "ברית bᵉrît obligation." In Ernst Jenni and Claus Westermann, eds., Mark E. Biddle, trans., *Theological Lexicon of the Old Testament*, 256–66. Peabody, Mass.: Hendrickson, 1997.

Lehne, Susanne. *The New Covenant in Hebrews*. JSNTSup 44. Sheffield: JSOT Press, 1990.

Levinson, Bernard M. *Deuteronomy and the Hermeneutics of Legal Innovation*. New York/Oxford: Oxford University Press, 1997.

Liao, Paul Shang-Hsin. *The Place of Covenant in the Theology of the Apostle Paul*. Unpublished Ph.D. dissertation. Hartford Seminary, 1973.

Lindars, Barnabas. *The Theology of the Letter to the Hebrews*. Cambridge: Cambridge University Press, 1991.

Lohfink, Norbert. *The Covenant Never Revoked: Biblical Reflections on Christian-Jewish Dialogue*. New York/Mahwah, N.J.: Paulist Press, 1991.

Martin, Ralph P. *2 Corinthians*. WBC 40. Waco, Tex.: Word, 1986.

Mayes, A. D. H. *Deuteronomy*. NCB. Greenwood, S.C.: Attic, 1979.

Mays, James Luther. *Hosea: A Commentary*. OTL. Philadelphia: Westminster Press, 1969.

McBride, S. Dean. *The Deuteronomic Name Theology*. Ph.D. dissertation. Harvard University, 1969.

McCarter, P. Kyle. *II Samuel*. AB 9. Garden City, N.Y.: Doubleday, 1984.

McCarthy, Dennis J. *Treaty and Covenant: A Study in Form in the Ancient Oriental Documents and in the Old Testament*. 2d ed. AnBib 21A. Rome: Pontifical Biblical Institute, 1978.

McConville, Gordon J. "ברית bᵉrîth" In W. A. VanGemeren, ed., *New International Dictionary of Old Testament Theology & Exegesis*, 747–55. Grand Rapids, Mich: Zondervan, 1997.

McKane, William. *A Critical and Exegetical Commentary on Jeremiah*. Vol. 2, *Jeremiah XXVI–LII*. ICC. Edinburgh: T. & T. Clark, 1996.

McKenzie, Steven L. "The Church in 1 John." *RQ* 19 (1976): 211–16.

————. "Deuteronomistic History, The." In David Noel Freedman, ed., *The Anchor Bible Dictionary,* 6 vols., 2:160–168. New York: Doubleday, 1992.

————. *All God's Children: A Biblical Critique of Racism.* Louisville, Ky.: Westminster John Knox Press, 1997.

————. "Why Didn't God Let David Build the Temple? The History of a Biblical Tradition." In M. Patrick Graham, Rick R. Marrs, and Steven L. McKenzie, eds., *Worship in the Old Testament: Essays in Honour of John T. Willis,* 204–24. JSOTSup 284. Sheffield: Sheffield Academic Press, 1998.

Mendenhall, George E. "Covenant Forms in Israelite Tradition." *BA* 17 (1954): 49–76.

Mettinger, Tryggve N. D. *King and Messiah: The Civil and Sacral Legitimation of the Israelite Kings.* ConBOT 8. Lund: C. W. K. Gleerup, 1976.

————. *The Dethronement of Sabaoth: Studies in the Shem and Kabod Theologies.* ConBOT 18. Lund: C. W. K. Gleerup, 1978.

Metger, Bruce M., and Michael D. Coogan, eds. *The Oxford Companion to the Bible.* New York: Oxford University Press, 1993.

Murphy-O'Connor, Jerome. *The Theology of the Second Letter to the Corinthians.* Cambridge: Cambridge University Press, 1991.

Murray, J. "Covenant." In J. D. Douglas, ed., *The New Bible Dictionary,* 264–69. Grand Rapids, Mich.: Eerdmans, 1967.

Nelson, Richard D. *Joshua: A Commentary.* OTL. Louisville, Ky.: Westminster John Knox Press, 1997.

Nicholson, Ernest W. *Deuteronomy and Tradition.* Philadelphia: Fortress Press, 1967.

————. The Decalogue as the Direct Address of God. *VT* 27 (1977): 422–33.

————. *God and His People. Covenant and Theology in the Old Testament.* Oxford: Clarendon Press, 1986.

Noth, Martin. *The Deuteronomistic History.* JSOTSup 15. 2d ed. Sheffield: Sheffield Academic Press, 1991.

Oden, Robert A. "The Place of Covenant in the Religion of Israel." In Patrick D. Miller, Jr., Paul D. Hanson, and S. Dean McBride, eds., *Ancient Israelite Religion: Essays in Honor of Frank Moore Cross,* 429–47. Philadelphia: Fortress Press, 1987.

Perlitt, Lothar. *Bundestheologie im Alten Testament.* WMANT 36. Neukirchen: Neukirchener Verlag, 1969.

von Rad, Gerhard. *Studies in Deuteronomy.* Trans. D. M. Stalker. SBT. Chicago: Henry Regnery, 1953.

———. *Deuteronomy: A Commentary.* OTL. Philadelphia: Westminster Press, 1966.

Rendtorff, Rolf. *Canon and Theology: Overtures to an Old Testament Theology.* Trans. and ed. Margaret Kohl. OBT. Minneapolis: Fortress Press, 1993.

Römer, Thomas C. *Israels Väter: Untersuchungen zur Väterthematik im Deuteronomium und in der deuteronomistischen Tradition.* OBO 99. Freiburg/Göttingen: Universitätsverlag/Vandenhoeck & Ruprecht, 1990.

———. "The Book of Deuteronomy." In Steven L. McKenzie and M. Patrick Graham, eds., *The History of Israel's Traditions: The Heritage of Martin Noth,* 178–212. JSOTSup 182. Sheffield: Sheffield Academic Press, 1994.

———. "Transformations in Deuteronomistic Biblical Historiography: On Book-Finding and Other Literary Strategies." *ZAW* 109 (1997): 1–11.

Sakenfeld, Katherine Doob. *The Meaning of Hesed in the Hebrew Bible: A New Inquiry.* HSM 17. Missoula, Mont.: Scholars Press, 1978.

———. *Faithfulness in Action: Loyalty in Biblical Perspective.* OBT. Philadelphia: Fortress Press, 1985.

———. "Love (OT)." In David Noel Freedman, ed., *The Anchor Bible Dictionary,* 6 vols., 4:375–81. New York: Doubleday, 1992.

Schniedewind, William M. *Society and the Promise to David: The Reception History of 2 Samuel 7: 1–17.* New York/Oxford: Oxford University Press, 1999.

Stager, Lawrence E. "The Archaeology of the Family in Ancient Israel." *BASOR* 260 (1985): 1–29.

———. "The Song of Deborah: Why Some Tribes Answered the Call and Others Did Not." *BAR* 15, no. 1 (Jan./Feb. 1989): 51–64.

Stamm, J. J. *The Ten Commandments in Recent Research.* SBT. Naperville, Ill.: Allenson, 1967.

Streete, Gail P. C. "Redaction Criticism." In Steven L. McKenzie and Stephen R. Haynes, eds., *To Each Its Own Meaning: Biblical Criticisms and Their Interpretation,* rev. ed., 105–21. Louisville, Ky.: Westminster John Knox Press, 1999.

Thrall, Margaret E. *The Second Epistle to the Corinthians.* Vol. 1, *Introduction and Commentary on II Corinthians I–VII.* ICC. Edinburgh: T. & T. Clark, 1994.

Van Seters, John. *Abraham in History and Tradition.* New Haven/London: Yale University Press, 1975.

———. *The Life of Moses: The Yahwist as Historian in Exodus–Numbers.* Louisville, Ky.: Westminster/John Knox Press, 1994.

———. "The Pentateuch." In Steven L. McKenzie and M. Patrick Graham, eds., *The Hebrew Bible Today: An Introduction to Critical Issues,* 31–49. Louisville, Ky.: Westminster John Knox Press, 1998.

Veijola, Timo. *Verheissung in der Krise: Studien zur Literatur und Theologie der Exilszeit anhand des 89. Psalms.* AASF B 220. Helsinki: Suomalainen Tiedeakatemia, 1992.

Viviano, Pauline A. "Source Criticism." In Steven L. McKenzie and Stephen R. Haynes, eds., *To Each Its Own Meaning: An Introduction to Biblical Criticisms and Their Application,* rev. ed., 35–57. Louisville, Ky.: Westminster John Knox Press, 1999.

Weinfeld, Moshe. "Deuteronomy: The Present State of Inquiry." *JBL* 86 (1967): 249–62.

————. "The Covenant of Grant in the Old Testament and in the Ancient Near East." *JAOS* 90 (1970): 184–203.

————. *Deuteronomy and the Deuteronomic School.* Oxford: Clarendon Press, 1972.

————. "ברית bᵉrîth." In G. Johannes Botterweck and Helmer Ringgren, eds., John T. Willis and David Green, trans., *Theological Dictionary of the Old Testament*, 9 vols., 2:253–79.Grand Rapids, Mich.: Eerdmans, 1974–1998.

————. *Deuteronomy 1–11: A New Translation with Introduction and Commentary.* AB 5. New York: Doubleday, 1991.

————. "Deuteronomy, Book of." In David Noel Freedman, ed., *The Anchor Bible Dictionary*, 6 vols., 2:168–83. New York: Doubleday, 1992.

Wellhausen, Julius. *Prolegomena to the History of Ancient Israel.* Gloucester, Mass.: Peter Smith, 1957.

de Wette, W. M. L. *Dissertatio critico-exegetica qua Deuteronomium a prioribus Pentateuchi libris diversum, alius cuiusdam recentioris auctoris opus esse monstratur.* Jena, 1805.

Williams, Sam K. *Galatians.* ANTC. Nashville: Abingdon Press, 1997.

Wiseman, D. J. "The Vassal Treaties of Esarhaddon." *Iraq* 20 (1858): 1–99.

Scripture Index

153